WHAT IS THE BOOK OF 2 KINGS?

Kids' Guides to God's Word Series

What Is the Book of Genesis?
What Is the Book of Exodus?
What Is the Book of Leviticus?
What Is the Book of Numbers?
What Is the Book of Deuteronomy?
What Is the Book of Joshua?
What Is the Book of Judges?
What Is the Book of Ruth?
What Is the Book of 1 Samuel?
What Is the Book of 2 Samuel?
What Is the Book of 1 Kings?
What Is the Book of 2 Kings?
What Are the Books of 1–2 Chronicles?
What Are the Books of Ezra & Nehemiah?
What Is the Book of Esther?
What Is the Book of Job?
What Is the Book of Psalms?
What Is the Book of Proverbs?
What Is the Book of Ecclesiastes?
What Are the Books of Song of Songs & Lamentations?
What Is the Book of Isaiah?
What Is the Book of Jeremiah?
What Is the Book of Ezekiel?
What Is the Book of Daniel?
What Are the Books of Hosea–Micah?
What Are the Books of Nahum–Malachi?
What Is the Gospel of Matthew?
What Is the Gospel of Mark?
What Is the Gospel of Luke?
What Is the Gospel of John?
What Is the Book of Acts?
What Is the Book of Romans?
What Is the Book of 1 Corinthians?
What Is the Book of 2 Corinthians?
What Is the Book of Galatians?
What Is the Book of Ephesians?
What Is the Book of Philippians?
What Are the Books of Colossians & Philemon?
What Are the Books of 1–2 Thessalonians?
What Are the Books of 1–2 Timothy & Titus?
What Is the Book of Hebrews?
What Is the Book of James?
What Are the Books of 1–2 Peter & Jude?
What Are the Books of 1-3 John?
What Is the Book of Revelation?

What Is the Book of

2 KINGS?

Michael Whitworth

ISBN 978-1-971767-18-5

Published by Start2Finish
Bend, Oregon 97702
start2finish.org

Printed in the United States of America

30 29 28 27 26 1 2 3 4 5

CONTENTS

INTRODUCTION

Have you ever watched a building being demolished? Not in person, necessarily, but maybe in one of those videos where engineers plant explosives on every floor of a skyscraper, and then someone pushes a button. For a second, nothing happens. Then the building shudders. The walls buckle. And in a matter of seconds, something that took years to construct collapses into a cloud of dust and rubble.

Here's the thing about demolitions: the building doesn't fall because of the explosion. The explosion just finishes what's already been weakened. By the time anyone pushes that button, the structure has been hollowed out from the inside. The collapse looks sudden, but it was a long time coming.

That's the book of 2 Kings. It's the story of two kingdoms that looked solid from the outside but had been rotting from within for generations. And by the last chapter, both of them are rubble.

WHY 2 KINGS MATTERS

Second Kings is not a feel-good book. If you're looking for victories and happy endings, you will find a few here, but they won't last. This is the book where the northern kingdom of Israel is conquered by Assyria, its people scattered across a foreign empire and never heard from again. This is the book where the southern kingdom of Judah is conquered by Babylon, its capital burned, its temple destroyed, and its people dragged into exile. This is the book where everything the Israelites had built since the days of Joshua comes crashing down.

So why read it?

Because 2 Kings answers one of the most important questions you'll ever face: What happens when people keep ignoring God? Not once or twice, but for generations? What does it look like when a nation has every warning, every chance, every reason to turn back, and still refuses?

And because 2 Kings answers another question too, one that matters even more: Does God give up?

The answer to the first question will sober you. The answer to the second will give you hope.

WHERE WE'VE BEEN

If you've been following the story of Israel through the Old Testament, you know things have been complicated for a long time. God chose Abraham and promised to make his descendants into a great nation. That family grew in Egypt, was enslaved for four hundred years, and then was rescued by God through Moses. God gave them his law, led them through the wilderness, and brought them into the Promised Land under Joshua.

Things went well for a while. Then they didn't. The book of Judges tells the ugly story of Israel spiraling through cycles of rebellion, suffering, and rescue. The people demanded a king.

God gave them Saul, who started strong and ended badly. Then came David, the shepherd king, the man after God's own heart, who united the nation and received God's promise of an everlasting dynasty. Solomon followed David and built the magnificent temple in Jerusalem, but his love for foreign wives and foreign gods cracked the foundation.

After Solomon's death, the kingdom split in two. Ten tribes formed the northern kingdom (called Israel), and two tribes formed the southern kingdom (called Judah). First Kings tells the story of that split and introduces the two great forces that dominate the rest of the story: the line of Jeroboam, whose counterfeit worship system poisoned the north from its very first day, and the line of David, whose covenant with God kept the south alive through one crisis after another.

First Kings also introduces the prophet Elijah, who stood alone against King Ahab and Queen Jezebel and their campaign to replace the worship of God with the worship of Baal. By the end of 1 Kings, Ahab is dead, but his family still rules the north, and Baal worship is still a cancer eating at both kingdoms.

Second Kings picks up the story right there.

WHAT YOU'RE ABOUT TO READ

The book of 2 Kings covers roughly three hundred years, from around 850 BC to the destruction of Jerusalem in 587 BC. Here's a roadmap of what's ahead.

Chapters 1–8 follow the prophets Elijah and Elisha. You'll watch Elijah leave the earth in a chariot of fire and see Elisha take up his mantle. Elisha's ministry is full of miracles:

multiplying oil for a widow, raising a dead boy, healing a foreign general, feeding a hundred men with a handful of bread, blinding an enemy army with a prayer. Through it all, God is proving that his power hasn't left Israel, even while Israel's kings refuse to follow him.

Chapters 9–10 tell the story of Jehu's violent revolution. God uses Jehu to destroy the house of Ahab and wipe out Baal worship in Israel. But Jehu's zeal has limits. He tears down Baal's temple but keeps the golden calves. His revolution changes the government but not the nation's heart.

Chapters 11–12 shift south to Judah, where the wicked queen Athaliah tries to destroy the entire royal family. One baby survives, hidden in the temple for six years. When he's crowned at age seven, the line of David continues by the thinnest possible thread.

Chapters 13–17 trace the long decline and fall of the northern kingdom. Kings rise and fall. Conspiracies pile up. Prophets warn. Nobody listens. And in 722 BC, Assyria conquers Samaria and scatters the ten northern tribes. The writer of Kings pauses to deliver a devastating explanation: this happened because Israel refused, generation after generation, to listen to God.

Chapters 18–20 are the brightest spot in the book. Hezekiah, king of Judah, trusts God in a way no king before or after him matches. When the Assyrian army surrounds Jerusalem and mocks the God of Israel, Hezekiah prays, and God destroys 185,000 enemy soldiers in a single night. But even Hezekiah stumbles, and his foolish decision to show off his treasures to Babylonian envoys plants the seed for Judah's future destruction.

Chapters 21–25 tell the final, heartbreaking chapter. Manasseh, Hezekiah's son, becomes the worst king in Judah's history and pushes the nation past the point of no return. Josiah, his grandson, launches the greatest reformation the nation has ever seen, but it comes too late. After Josiah's death, four final kings lead Judah into the ground. Babylon destroys Jerusalem, burns the temple, and carries the people into exile. The book ends with a whisper of hope: a Davidic king, still alive, still called "king of Judah," eating at a table in Babylon.

BEFORE YOU BEGIN

A few things to keep in mind as you read. The violence is real. Wars, assassinations, sieges, child sacrifice, even cannibalism show up in these chapters. The Bible doesn't sanitize what happened. It shows you the full cost of sin and the devastating consequences of abandoning God. These aren't comfortable passages, but they're honest.

The politics are complicated. Two kingdoms running side by side, with overlapping king lists and intermarrying royal families, can get confusing. Don't worry about memorizing every name. Focus on the patterns: faithfulness leads to blessing, rebellion leads to ruin, and God's word always comes true.

This book points to Jesus. The line of David survives assassination attempts, exile, and everything in between. It survives because God made a promise, and God keeps his promises. That line runs from David through Hezekiah and Josiah, through the exile and beyond, all the way to a manger in Bethlehem. Second Kings shows you why a Savior was necessary. Every king, even the best ones, eventually fails. The story is waiting for a King who won't.

LET'S BEGIN

So here we are, standing at the beginning of the end. Two kingdoms that should have been one. A God who keeps sending prophets to people who keep refusing to listen. A covenant promise that looks more impossible with every passing chapter. And a story that will take you from chariots of fire to the smoking ruins of Jerusalem.

It's not a comfortable ride. But it's an important one. Because the God who speaks in 2 Kings is the same God who speaks today. And if this book teaches you anything, it will teach you this: you can ignore him, but you can't escape him. You can walk away from him, but he will not walk away from you. And even when everything collapses, even when the temple is ash and the city is rubble and the people are gone, he will find a way to keep his promise.

He always does.

1

WHEN THE PROPHET LEAVES

At the end of *Frozen 2*, something unexpected happens. Elsa doesn't come back to rule Arendelle. She stays in the enchanted forest, where she belongs, and Anna—who has spent most of the movie feeling like she's not enough—becomes queen. There's no magical ceremony. No dramatic crowning moment. Just Anna, standing in the place her sister used to stand, realizing that the kingdom needs her now. She didn't ask for this. She's not sure she's ready. But Elsa is gone, and someone has to lead.

Now imagine that feeling, but the stakes are infinitely higher. The person leaving isn't a queen; he's the most powerful prophet Israel has ever known. A man who called down fire from heaven, outran chariots, and stood alone against an entire nation's worth of false religion. For decades, Elijah had been the one standing between Israel and total spiritual collapse. He was, as one person put it, worth more to the nation than an entire army.

And now he's about to leave.

That's where 2 Kings begins. The first three chapters tell the story of a dramatic transition from one prophet to another, from one era to the next. Elijah takes his final stand, Elisha picks up where he left off, and a faithless king discovers that God's power didn't leave when Elijah did.

THE KING WHO FORGOT GOD

Before Elijah leaves, he has one last confrontation. King Ahaziah, son of the infamous Ahab and Jezebel, had fallen through a lattice on the upper floor of his palace in Samaria and injured himself badly. It was serious enough that Ahaziah wasn't sure he'd survive. So he sent messengers to get help.

But here's the thing: he didn't send them to God. He sent them to a pagan deity called Baal-Zebub, a god worshiped in the Philistine city of Ekron, about forty-five miles away. The king of Israel—the nation God had rescued from Egypt, led through the wilderness, and established in the Promised Land—sent his servants to ask a foreign idol whether he would recover from his injuries.

Think about what that means. It's not like Ahaziah had never heard of the God of Israel. He'd grown up watching his father Ahab go toe-to-toe with Elijah. He'd seen what happened on Mount Carmel, where fire from heaven proved that the Lord alone was God. He knew. He just didn't care. He had chosen Baal, just like his parents before him—not out of ignorance, but out of preference.

God intercepted the mission. He sent Elijah to meet Ahaziah's messengers on the road with a devastating question: "Is it because there is no God in Israel that you're going to consult Baal-Zebub?" And then came the judgment: "You will not leave the bed you're lying on. You will certainly die."

The messengers turned around and reported back to the king. Ahaziah knew immediately who had stopped them. A hairy man in a leather belt? That was Elijah.

FIRE FROM HEAVEN—AGAIN

Instead of repenting, Ahaziah sent soldiers. A captain and fifty men marched up to where Elijah was sitting on a hilltop and ordered him to come down. "Man of God," the captain said, "the king says, 'Come down!'"

Elijah's response was calm and terrifying: "If I am a man of God, may fire come down from heaven and consume you and your fifty men." Fire fell. They were gone.

Ahaziah sent another captain with another fifty men. Same demand. Same result. More fire. More death.

This might seem extreme. But think about what Ahaziah was actually doing. He wasn't inviting Elijah to a polite conversation. He was sending armed soldiers to arrest (and likely kill) God's prophet. He was trying to silence God's word by force. The fire wasn't random cruelty. It was God defending his messenger and proving, one more time, that no king is powerful enough to shut God up.

A third captain came. But this one was different. He didn't strut up the hill barking orders. He fell on his knees. "Man of God," he begged, "please have respect for my life and the lives of these fifty men." He had seen what happened to the others. He was terrified. And his terror saved him.

God told Elijah to go with him. So Elijah walked into the palace, stood before the injured king, and delivered the same message face to face: "Because you sent messengers to consult

Baal-Zebub, as if there were no God in Israel, you will not leave that bed. You will die."

And he did. Ahaziah died according to the word of the Lord.

Here's what's haunting about Ahaziah's story: the only thing recorded about his reign is how he died. We know nothing else about him—no achievements, no policies, no legacy. Just that in the most critical moment of his life, he turned to a god that couldn't help him instead of the God who could. That's his entire biography. It's both sad and stupid. And it's a warning.

THE DAY ELIJAH LEFT

With Ahaziah dead, the story shifts to something that had been coming for a long time. God was about to take Elijah off the earth—not through death, but through something no one had ever seen before.

Everybody seemed to know it was happening. Elijah knew. Elisha knew. Groups of prophets in Bethel and Jericho pulled Elisha aside and whispered, "Do you know the Lord is going to take your master from you today?" Each time, Elisha gave the same tight-lipped answer: "Yes, I know. Be quiet."

There's a quiet dread in this scene. Elijah kept telling Elisha to stay behind—at Gilgal, at Bethel, at Jericho. Each time, Elisha refused: "As surely as the Lord lives and as you live, I will not leave you." He was not letting go. Not yet.

They walked together to the Jordan River. Fifty prophets followed at a distance and watched. Elijah took his cloak, rolled it up, and struck the water. The Jordan divided, just like it had for Joshua and the Israelites centuries earlier when they first entered the Promised Land. The two prophets crossed over on dry ground.

On the other side, Elijah turned to his apprentice. "Tell me, what can I do for you before I am taken?"

Elisha's request was bold: "Let me inherit a double portion of your spirit." He wasn't asking to be twice as powerful as Elijah. In Israel's inheritance law, the firstborn son received a double portion of the father's estate. Elisha was asking to be recognized as Elijah's true successor, the one who would carry on his work.

"You've asked a difficult thing," Elijah said. "But if you see me when I am taken from you, it will be yours."

They kept walking. They kept talking. And then, without warning, a chariot of fire and horses of fire appeared between them, and Elijah was swept up to heaven in a whirlwind.

Elisha saw it. He cried out, "My father! My father! The chariots and horsemen of Israel!" Then Elijah was gone, and Elisha tore his clothes in grief.

The lion was dead. Or rather, the lion had been taken. And Elisha was standing alone on the east side of the Jordan, holding nothing but his mentor's fallen cloak and a prayer that God's power hadn't left with Elijah.

WHERE IS THE GOD OF ELIJAH?

Elisha picked up the cloak. He walked back to the Jordan and struck the water, asking the question that mattered more than anything else: "Where is the Lord, the God of Elijah?"

The water divided. Elisha crossed over on dry ground—just as Elijah had done minutes earlier. The watching prophets saw it and understood immediately: "The spirit of Elijah rests on Elisha."

This is the point. Elijah was extraordinary, but the power had never been Elijah's. It was God's. And God was still here. The instrument had changed, but the hand behind it hadn't.

What followed was a series of events that confirmed Elisha as God's new prophet. At Jericho, the city's water supply was contaminated, causing death and miscarriages among the people and their livestock. Jericho had been under a curse since Joshua's day, and that curse was still doing damage. Elisha threw salt into the spring and declared, "This is what the Lord says: 'I have healed this water. Never again will it cause death.'" The water was healed. The curse was broken. Grace had come to a place that had known nothing but judgment.

Then, on the road to Bethel—a city that had been a center of false worship for eighty years—a group of young men came out and mocked Elisha. "Go on up, you baldhead!" they jeered. They weren't innocent kids making fun of a bald guy. They were from a town hostile to God's prophets, and their taunting was a deliberate rejection of Elisha's authority. "Go up" may have been a mocking reference to Elijah's departure, as in, "Why don't you disappear too?" Elisha pronounced a curse in the name of the Lord, and two bears came out of the woods and mauled forty-two of them.

It's a hard story. But the writer includes it for a reason. Elisha's word carried the same weight as Elijah's. God's prophet could speak grace to Jericho and judgment to Bethel. The word of the Lord could heal or it could harm, and the difference depended on whether people received it or rejected it.

THREE KINGS AND A PROPHET

With Elisha established, the story turns to politics and a military disaster.

Joram, brother of the dead Ahaziah, became king of Israel. The writer's assessment is blunt: Joram did evil in the eyes of the Lord, though not as badly as his parents. He removed a sacred stone his father had set up for Baal worship. But he still clung to the religious system that Jeroboam had created generations earlier—the counterfeit worship centers that had been pulling Israel away from God since the kingdom split. Getting rid of the worst idol isn't the same as following God.

Joram's immediate problem was Moab. For years, the king of Moab had paid massive tribute to Israel: a hundred thousand lambs and the wool of a hundred thousand rams. But when Ahab died, Moab rebelled. Joram decided to fight back. He recruited Jehoshaphat, king of Judah, and the king of Edom, and the three armies marched south around the Dead Sea to attack Moab from below.

It was a disaster waiting to happen. After seven days of marching through desert, the army ran out of water. No water for the soldiers. No water for the animals. They were going to die before they ever reached the enemy.

Joram blamed God: "Has the Lord called us three kings together just to hand us over to Moab?" Notice what he did there—he only mentioned God when things went wrong. He hadn't sought God's guidance before launching this campaign. He hadn't consulted a prophet. But now that he was in trouble, suddenly it was God's fault.

Jehoshaphat, to his credit, asked the right question: "Is

there no prophet of the Lord here?" Someone mentioned Elisha. Jehoshaphat recognized the name. The three kings went down to see him.

Elisha did not roll out the welcome mat. He looked at Joram and said, essentially, "What do I have to do with you? Go ask your mother's prophets." When Joram protested, Elisha was brutally honest: "If it weren't for the presence of Jehoshaphat, I wouldn't even look at you."

This is important. Elisha helped Joram not because Joram deserved it but because of Jehoshaphat, the king of David's line. Joram received mercy because of someone else standing beside him. If that sounds familiar, it should. We receive mercy from God not because we deserve it, but because Jesus, the ultimate son of David, stands beside us.

Elisha called for a musician. While the music played, God's hand came upon him, and he prophesied: the valley would fill with water even though there would be no wind and no rain. And that was the easy part—God would also hand Moab over to them.

The next morning, water flowed in from the direction of Edom and filled the valley. When the Moabites saw the water reflecting the red morning sun, they thought it was blood. They assumed the three allied armies had turned on each other. "To the plunder!" they shouted—and charged straight into an ambush. Israel routed them completely.

But the story ends on a dark note. Cornered in his last stronghold, the king of Moab took his own firstborn son—the crown prince—and sacrificed him on the city wall as a burnt offering to his god. The horror of that act caused the Israelite coalition to withdraw. They went home with a victory that felt incomplete.

The contrast couldn't be sharper. Israel had a God who spoke, who provided water from nowhere, who gave victory without being bribed. Moab had a god who demanded the blood of children and still couldn't save them. One God speaks. The other devours. That's the difference between the Lord and every idol that has ever existed.

WHAT THIS MEANS FOR US

First, where you turn in a crisis reveals what you really believe. Ahaziah's instinct in his worst moment was to reach for Baal, not God. Our instincts in hard times reveal the same thing. When everything falls apart, who do you run to first? What you reach for in a crisis tells you more about your faith than anything you say on a normal day.

Second, God's work doesn't depend on one person. Elijah was irreplaceable—except that God replaced him. The power was never Elijah's to begin with. It was God's, and God gave it to Elisha just as freely. If you've ever lost someone important—a parent, a mentor, a minister, a friend who helped you follow God—know this: the God of Elijah is still here.

Third, partial obedience is still disobedience. Joram removed his father's Baal stone but clung to Jeroboam's false worship. He cleaned up the worst of it and called it enough. God never calls partial obedience enough. He wants all of you, not just the parts you're comfortable surrendering.

Fourth, we receive mercy because of another. Joram didn't deserve God's help. He got it because Jehoshaphat was standing next to him. In the same way, we don't deserve God's grace. We receive it because Jesus stands beside us. Every good thing God gives you comes not because of your merit but because of his Son.

TALKING POINTS

1. **Ahaziah sent messengers to a pagan god instead of turning to the God of Israel.** What are some things people turn to today instead of God when they're scared or hurting? Why do you think we sometimes look for answers everywhere except from God?

2. **Elisha refused to leave Elijah's side, even when Elijah told him to stay behind.** What does Elisha's loyalty tell us about how we should treat the people who are mentoring and teaching us? How can we show that kind of faithfulness?

3. **When Elisha struck the Jordan with Elijah's cloak, the water parted, proving that God's power hadn't left with Elijah.** Have you ever gone through a transition where you weren't sure God was still with you? What helped you trust that he was?

4. **Elisha healed the water at Jericho but pronounced judgment near Bethel.** What does this tell us about how God's word works—that it can bring both blessing and consequences depending on how people respond to it?

5. **Joram only thought about God when he was in trouble. Elisha called him out for it.** Why is it a problem to treat God like an emergency exit instead of someone you walk with every day? How can we avoid falling into that pattern?

Elijah was gone. But the God of Elijah was very much still at work—through a new prophet, in a new era, with the same unstoppable power. And Elisha was just getting started. The miracles were about to multiply in ways no one expected.

Turn the page.

2

THE GOD WHO SHOWS UP

In *Cinderella*, the girl who needs rescuing the most is the one nobody notices. She sleeps in the attic. She scrubs the floors. Her stepsisters get the gowns and the attention while she gets the ashes and the orders. When the invitation to the royal ball arrives, Cinderella has nothing. No dress. No carriage. No way to get there. Her situation is completely hopeless.

And then help comes from the strangest possible place. A fairy godmother turns a pumpkin into a coach. Mice become horses. A ragged dress becomes a gown. The most ordinary, overlooked things in Cinderella's world become the instruments of her transformation. Nobody saw it coming. Nobody would have guessed that the girl covered in cinders would be the one dancing with the prince before midnight.

The whole story turns on this idea: what looks like nothing in the right hands becomes everything.

Second Kings 4–5 are packed with people who need something they cannot get on their own. A widow drowning in debt. A wealthy woman whose son has died in her arms. A group of prophets staring at a pot of poisoned stew. A hundred hungry men with not nearly enough food. And a foreign general covered in a skin disease that all his power and money can't cure.

In every case, God shows up. But almost never the way anyone expects. He takes a jar of oil that represents a widow's poverty and turns it into her provision. He uses flour to neutralize a deadly pot of stew. He feeds a hundred men with twenty loaves that shouldn't have been enough. He heals the most powerful general in the region through a muddy river and a command that seemed beneath the man's dignity. And the person who sets the whole Naaman story in motion isn't a king or a priest. It's a captured slave girl that nobody thought mattered.

Pumpkins into coaches. Oil into an ocean. A river into a cure. God has always done his best work with the things everyone else overlooks.

A JAR OF OIL AND AN OCEAN OF DEBT

The first story in chapter 4 is brief but devastating. A widow comes to Elisha in a panic. Her husband had been a faithful follower of God, one of the prophets in Elisha's circle, and now he's dead. Worse, he left behind debts so large that the creditor is coming to take her two sons as slaves. In the ancient world, this was legal. If you couldn't pay, your children could be seized to work off what you owed.

Put yourself in her place. She's already lost her husband. Now she's about to lose her boys. And the bitter twist is that her husband wasn't some crook who ran up debts through reckless living. He was a man who feared God. Sometimes the people who suffer most are the people who've been most faithful. The widow doesn't pretend to understand why. She just brings her problem to the man of God and lays it at his feet.

Elisha asks her one question: "What do you have in your house?"

Almost nothing, she says. Just a small jar of oil.

Elisha tells her to go borrow as many empty jars as she can find from her neighbors. Then shut the door and start pouring. The widow obeys. She pours oil from that one little jar into container after container, and the oil keeps flowing until every single jar is full. Then it stops.

Elisha tells her to sell the oil, pay off the debt, and live on what's left over. God didn't just solve her immediate crisis. He provided for her future. The jar that symbolized how little she had became the instrument of how much God gave.

A SON GIVEN, A SON TAKEN, A SON RESTORED

The next story is longer and harder. A wealthy woman in the town of Shunem regularly hosted Elisha when he traveled through the area. She even built a small room on her roof so the prophet would have a place to stay. She wasn't doing it for a reward. She simply recognized that Elisha was a holy man of God and wanted to help.

Elisha wanted to repay her kindness. He asked what she needed. She said nothing. But Elisha's servant Gehazi pointed out something she hadn't mentioned: she had no son, and her husband was old. In the ancient world, having no children meant having no one to care for you in old age and no one to carry on your family's name.

Elisha made a promise: "About this time next year, you will

hold a son in your arms." The woman's reaction wasn't excitement. It was fear. "Don't mislead me," she said. She didn't want to hope for something that wouldn't come true.

But it did. The boy was born, just as Elisha said. He grew. And then one day, out in the fields with his father, the boy grabbed his head and cried out in pain. They carried him to his mother. He sat on her lap until noon. And then he died.

The woman didn't scream. She didn't collapse. She laid her son on Elisha's bed, saddled a donkey, and rode as fast as she could to find the prophet at Mount Carmel, about fifteen miles away. When her husband asked why she was going, she gave an evasive answer. When Gehazi ran out to ask if everything was all right, she brushed him off. She wasn't going to talk to anyone except the man who had made the promise.

When she reached Elisha, she grabbed his feet and poured out her anguish: "Did I ask you for a son? Didn't I tell you not to raise my hopes?"

This is the hardest part of the story. God gave her a gift she hadn't asked for, and then it was taken away. The joy made the grief worse, because now she had something to lose. This is one of the rawest moments in the Old Testament. The Bible doesn't pretend that following God protects you from devastating loss. It shows you real people in real pain, clinging to a God they don't understand.

Elisha went to the boy. He prayed. He lay on the child, mouth to mouth, eyes to eyes, hands to hands. The boy's body grew warm. Elisha got up, paced the room, lay on him again. The boy sneezed seven times and opened his eyes.

The child was alive. God had given, God had allowed

death, and God had restored. It's a preview of what God will ultimately do for all his people. Death is real, but it doesn't get the final word. This woman's story, set in a small house in an obscure village, carries a promise that echoes all the way to the resurrection.

STEW, BREAD, AND THE GOD OF DAILY NEEDS

Two shorter episodes follow, and both deal with something as basic as food.

In the first, Elisha's group of prophets is gathered during a famine. Someone goes out to collect herbs for a pot of stew, comes back with wild gourds he doesn't recognize, and chops them into the pot. One bite, and the men are gagging. "There is death in the pot!" they shout. Whatever he'd picked was either poisonous or so bitter it was inedible. Elisha threw flour into the pot and the stew became harmless.

In the second, a man brings Elisha twenty loaves of barley bread and some fresh grain. It's a generous gift, but there are a hundred men to feed. Elisha's servant is incredulous: "How can I set this before a hundred men?" Elisha insists. "Give it to the people to eat. For this is what the Lord says: 'They will eat and have some left over.'" They did. And there was food to spare.

These stories might seem small compared to raising a dead child. But that's precisely the point. God doesn't just show up for the spectacular moments. He cares about poisoned stew and not enough bread. He cares about the ordinary crises that make up most of life. The widow needed money. The Shunammite needed her son back. The prophets needed safe food and enough of it. God met every single need.

If that pattern sounds familiar, it should. Centuries later, Jesus would feed thousands with a few loaves and fish, with baskets of leftovers. He was doing what Elisha did, but on a scale that made it clear: a greater than Elisha is here.

THE GENERAL WHO ALMOST MISSED HIS HEALING

And now we come to one of the most important stories in the entire Old Testament.

Naaman was commander of the army of Aram (modern-day Syria). He was famous, decorated, respected by his king, and feared by his enemies. The text says something remarkable about him: "Through him the Lord had given victory to Aram." Even though Naaman didn't know it, the God of Israel was the one behind his success.

But Naaman had a problem no amount of military glory could solve. He had a serious skin disease. The Bible calls it leprosy, though it may not have been exactly what we think of by that name today. Whatever it was, it was severe enough to be a source of real suffering and social stigma.

The solution came from the last person you'd expect. A young Israelite girl, captured in a raid and forced into slavery in Naaman's household, mentioned to her mistress that there was a prophet in Israel who could heal her master. Think about what that means. This girl had been ripped from her home, her family, her country. She had every reason to hate Naaman and his people. Instead, she cared enough to point him toward God. The whole story hangs on the faith of a child nobody thought mattered.

Naaman took the girl's advice and traveled to Israel with a letter from his king, a massive amount of silver and gold, and ten sets of clothing. He went first to the king of Israel, who panicked. "Am I God? Can I kill and bring back to life?" The king had no idea what to do.

Elisha sent word: "Have the man come to me and he will know that there is a prophet in Israel." So Naaman rolled up to Elisha's house with his horses and chariots, expecting the full treatment. He figured the prophet would come out, call on his God's name, wave his hand over the diseased skin, and heal him right there.

That's not what happened. Elisha didn't even come to the door. He sent a messenger with a simple instruction: "Go, wash yourself seven times in the Jordan, and your flesh will be restored."

Naaman was furious. He had expected something dramatic, something worthy of a man of his stature. Instead he got a secondhand message telling him to take a bath in a muddy river. "Aren't the rivers of Damascus better than all the waters of Israel?" he fumed. He turned around and started to leave.

This is the moment the story almost ended in tragedy. Naaman nearly walked away from his healing because it didn't look the way he thought it should.

His servants saved him. They said something so simple it's almost funny: "If the prophet had told you to do some great thing, wouldn't you have done it? How much more, then, when he tells you, 'Wash and be cleansed'!" In other words: You came all this way. Just try it.

Naaman swallowed his pride, went down to the Jordan, and dipped himself seven times. When he came up the seventh time, his skin was clean. Completely restored, like the skin of a young boy. The great man had to become small. The commander had to take orders. The outsider had to trust a God he didn't know.

And when it was over, Naaman came back to Elisha and made one of the greatest confessions of faith in the entire Bible: "Now I know that there is no God in all the world except in Israel."

THE SERVANT WHO RUINED EVERYTHING

But the story doesn't end there. It has a dark conclusion. Gehazi, Elisha's servant, had watched the whole thing. He saw Naaman offer Elisha gifts. He saw Elisha refuse them. Elisha didn't take a single coin, because he wanted Naaman to understand something crucial: God's grace is free. You don't pay for it. You don't earn it. You don't bribe God into healing you. Grace is a gift, and Elisha's refusal was meant to teach Naaman the difference between the God of Israel and every other deity in the ancient world, the kind that always had their hands out, demanding offerings and sacrifices.

Gehazi didn't care about any of that. He ran after Naaman, made up a lie about two visiting prophets who needed silver and clothing, and collected the goods for himself. Then he hid them and went back to Elisha as if nothing had happened.

But Elisha knew. "Was not my spirit with you when the man got down from his chariot to meet you?" he asked. And then the judgment: "Naaman's leprosy will cling to you and to your descendants forever." Gehazi walked out of the room a leper.

The contrast is devastating. A pagan general believed and was healed. God's own servant lied and was struck with the very disease God had just removed. Naaman went home clean because he humbled himself. Gehazi went home diseased because he was greedy. The outsider received grace. The insider corrupted it.

Jesus pointed to exactly this story centuries later when the people of Nazareth rejected him. "There were many lepers in Israel in the time of Elisha the prophet," Jesus said, "and not one of them was cleansed, only Naaman the Syrian." That statement almost got Jesus killed. His audience understood the implication: God was willing to heal a foreigner while passing over his own people. Privilege doesn't guarantee anything.

WHAT THIS MEANS FOR US

First, God meets you where your need actually is. The widow needed money. The Shunammite needed her son. The prophets needed food. Naaman needed healing. God didn't offer generic help. He addressed each person's specific, concrete situation. Whatever you're struggling with right now, God sees the real need, not just the surface problem.

Second, God often works through unlikely people. A slave girl pointed Naaman to healing. Servants talked their master out of walking away from his cure. A man from an obscure town brought bread to the prophets. God doesn't need powerful people to accomplish his purposes. He regularly uses the overlooked, the underestimated, and the young.

Third, humility is the door to grace. Naaman almost missed his healing because his pride wouldn't let him do something simple and unglamorous. God's instructions don't always make sense to us. They don't always feel dignified. But the question is whether we trust God enough to obey even when we don't understand.

Fourth, God's grace cannot be bought. Elisha refused Naaman's gifts because grace that costs the recipient isn't grace at all. Gehazi tried to put a price tag on what God had given freely, and it cost him everything. This points straight to the gospel: salvation is a gift, not a transaction. You cannot earn it, and anyone who tells you otherwise is doing what Gehazi did.

TALKING POINTS

1. **The widow's husband had been faithful to God, and yet his family still faced financial disaster after his death.** Why do you think bad things happen to people who love God? How does the widow's decision to bring her problem to Elisha show us what to do when life doesn't seem fair?

2. **The Shunammite woman told Elisha, "Don't raise my hopes." She was afraid to believe something too good to be true.** Have you ever been afraid to hope for something because you didn't want to be disappointed? What does this story teach us about trusting God even when we're scared?

3. **Naaman expected a dramatic, impressive healing and almost walked away when God's instructions were simple.** Why do you think we sometimes want God to work in spectacular ways instead of trusting his simpler instructions? What areas of your life might God be asking you to simply obey?

4. **A captured slave girl, with every reason to be bitter, pointed Naaman toward God instead.** What does her attitude tell us about how God can use us even in situations that

feel unfair or painful? How can you be a witness for God in difficult circumstances?

5. **Gehazi saw an incredible miracle and his first thought was how to profit from it.** What warning does his story carry for people who grow up around faith but never let it change their hearts? How can we guard against taking God's grace for granted?

Debt, death, poison, hunger, disease. God's power wasn't limited to one category of need. Elisha's ministry was proving, miracle by miracle, that the God of Israel was an overflowing fountain of help for anyone willing to receive it. But the biggest test of all was coming. An entire city was about to be surrounded by an enemy army, and this time, Elisha himself would be the target.

Turn the page.

3

MORE THAN WHAT YOU SEE

Have you ever been in a situation where you were completely outnumbered? Maybe it was a dodgeball game where your whole team had been eliminated and you were the last one standing. Maybe it was a group project where everyone disagreed with your idea. Maybe it was just one of those days where it felt like the whole world was against you and you had nothing left.

In the movie *Mulan*, there is a moment like that. Mulan and her tiny group of soldiers crest a snowy ridge and find themselves face to face with the entire Hun army. Thousands of warriors on horseback, stretching across the horizon. There is no way to win this fight. The numbers are impossible. Every rational calculation says it's over.

But Mulan doesn't run. She grabs a cannon, aims it at the mountain above the army, and triggers an avalanche that buries the enemy. The thing that saved them wasn't superior numbers. It was seeing something no one else could see.

Second Kings 6–8 is about seeing what's really there. An invisible army on a hillside. A camp full of food that no one knows about. A God who is working behind the scenes when everything on the surface looks hopeless. These chapters take us from comedy to horror to heartbreak, but through it all, the same message keeps breaking through: the situation is never as desperate as it looks, because God is never as absent as he seems.

THE FLOATING AXE HEAD

The first story in chapter 6 is so short you might wonder why it's in the Bible at all. The group of prophets following Elisha needed more space, so they went to the Jordan River to cut down trees for a new meeting place. While one of them was chopping, the iron axe head flew off the handle and sank into the water. The man panicked. "Oh no, my master! It was borrowed!"

That might not sound like a crisis to us. But iron tools were expensive. This prophet was so poor he couldn't even afford his own axe. Losing a borrowed one meant debt he couldn't pay. Elisha cut a stick, threw it into the water, and the iron floated to the surface.

It's a tiny miracle. No armies are saved. No nations are rescued. Just one broke, scared man who needed his axe back. And God cared enough to do something about it. In the middle of chapters filled with wars and sieges and political intrigue, the Bible pauses to tell you that God notices the small stuff. Your problems don't have to be enormous to matter to him.

THE ARMY YOU CAN'T SEE

The next story is one of the most famous in the Old Testament, and it earns that reputation.

The king of Aram (Syria) was at war with Israel, and he kept losing. Every time he set an ambush, the Israelites avoided it. Every time he planned a surprise attack, Israel was ready. The king was furious. He accused his own officers of being traitors, leaking his plans to the enemy. But one of his servants told him the truth: "Elisha, the prophet who is in Israel, tells the king of Israel the very words you speak in your bedroom."

So the king of Aram did the logical thing. If Elisha was the problem, he would eliminate Elisha. He sent horses, chariots, and a large force to surround the city of Dothan, where Elisha was staying. They came at night. By morning, the city was encircled.

Elisha's servant woke up, walked outside, and saw the army. He ran back inside, terrified. "Oh no, my master! What shall we do?"

Elisha's answer is one of the greatest lines in Scripture: "Don't be afraid. Those who are with us are more than those who are with them."

The servant must have thought Elisha had lost his mind. He could count. There were two of them and an army outside. The math didn't work.

Then Elisha prayed: "Lord, open his eyes so he may see." And God opened the servant's eyes. The hills around Dothan were full of horses and chariots of fire. An invisible army, God's army, surrounded the army that surrounded Elisha. The servant had been looking at the situation with human eyes. He needed God's eyes.

What happened next is almost funny. As the Aramean soldiers closed in, Elisha prayed again, this time asking God to strike them with a kind of confusion or visual disorientation. God did. Then Elisha walked right up to the confused soldiers and said, "Follow me. I'll lead you to the man you're looking for." He led the entire army ten miles down the road, straight into the capital city of Samaria, right into the hands of the king of Israel.

When God opened the soldiers' eyes, they found themselves surrounded by the Israelite army. The king of Israel was giddy: "Shall I kill them? Shall I kill them?"

Elisha said no. Feed them. Give them a feast and send them home. So the king of Israel threw a banquet for the very army that had come to destroy God's prophet. The enemies of God's people sat down, ate bread and meat, and went home. And for a while, the raids stopped.

The Arameans had come to capture Elisha and ended up being captured by grace.

THE SIEGE THAT BROKE A CITY

But the peace didn't last. Ben-Hadad, king of Aram, eventually gathered his entire army and laid siege to Samaria. A siege is one of the cruelest forms of warfare. The attacking army doesn't storm the walls. It just waits. It surrounds the city so nothing can get in or out. No food. No supplies. No escape. The city slowly starves.

And Samaria starved. The famine became so severe that a donkey's head sold for an absurd amount of money. People were eating things that would make your stomach turn. Then it got worse. One day, as the king of Israel was walking along the wall, a woman cried out to him for help. When he asked what was wrong, she told him a story so horrifying it's hard to read. She and another woman had agreed to cook and eat their own children to survive. The first woman had given up her son. Now the second woman had hidden hers and wouldn't keep the bargain.

This is one of the darkest moments in the entire Bible. But the writer includes it for a reason. Centuries earlier, when God made his covenant with Israel, he had warned them that if they abandoned him, this exact nightmare would come. Starvation. Siege. Parents consuming their own children. It wasn't a random disaster. It was the consequence of a nation that had spent generations walking away from God.

The king was devastated. He tore his clothes and people could see he was wearing sackcloth underneath, a sign of mourning and desperation. But his response wasn't repentance. It was rage. He blamed Elisha and sent a man to cut off the prophet's head. He had been willing to wait on God for a while, but his patience was spent. "This disaster is from the Lord," he said. "Why should I wait for the Lord any longer?"

That question echoes through the centuries. When suffering drags on and God doesn't seem to answer, the temptation is always the same: give up, turn bitter, and decide God isn't worth trusting.

LEPERS, LEFTOVERS, AND A PROMISE KEPT

But Elisha had a word from God. He announced something that sounded insane: "About this time tomorrow, flour and barley will be selling at normal prices in the gate of Samaria." One of the king's officers laughed in his face. "Even if the Lord opened the windows of heaven, could this happen?" Elisha looked at him and said, "You will see it with your own eyes, but you will not eat any of it."

Then the story shifts to four men with skin diseases who were sitting outside the city gate. They were outcasts, stuck between the starving city and the enemy camp. They had nothing to lose. "If we sit here, we'll die," they reasoned. "If we go into the city, we'll die. If we surrender to the Arameans, they might kill us or they might let us live." So they walked toward the enemy camp at dusk.

When they arrived, the camp was empty. Tents, horses, donkeys, food, silver, gold, clothing. All of it sitting there, abandoned. The Arameans were gone.

Here's what had happened: "The Lord had caused the Aramean army to hear the sound of chariots and horses and a great army." The soldiers panicked, convinced that Israel had hired the armies of other nations to attack them. They fled for their lives, leaving everything behind. God didn't send a single Israelite soldier. He sent a sound. He used noise to rout an army and save a city.

The four men ate and drank and started hiding loot for themselves. Then their consciences kicked in. "We're not doing right," they said to each other. "This is a day of good news and we are keeping it to ourselves." So they went back to the city and told the gatekeepers. The gatekeepers told the king. The king, suspicious as always, thought it was a trap. But a nameless servant convinced him to send scouts to check.

The scouts confirmed it. The road was littered with equipment and clothing the Arameans had thrown away in their panic. The people of Samaria poured out of the city and plundered the camp. Flour and barley sold at exactly the prices Elisha had predicted.

And the officer who had mocked Elisha's promise? The king had put him in charge of the gate. When the starving crowd stampeded out to reach the food, they trampled him to death. He saw the deliverance with his own eyes, just as Elisha said. But he never tasted it.

KINDNESS, TEARS, AND THE COMING STORM

Chapter 8 ties up loose ends and sets the stage for what comes next.

First, we learn what happened to the Shunammite woman from chapter 4. Elisha had warned her about a seven-year famine and told her to leave the country. She obeyed and lived in Philistia until the famine ended. When she came back, someone had taken her land. She went to the king to beg for its return. And in one of those moments that can only be God's timing, she walked in just as Gehazi was telling the king the story of how Elisha had raised her son from the dead. The king was so struck by the coincidence that he ordered everything restored to her, including all the income from her land for the years she'd been gone.

God hadn't forgotten her. He'd been arranging the details long before she walked through that door.

Then comes a darker scene. Elisha traveled to Damascus, the capital of Aram. Ben-Hadad, the king, was sick and sent a man named Hazael to ask Elisha whether he would recover. Elisha's answer was strange: "Go tell him he will recover. But the Lord has shown me that he will in fact die." Then Elisha stared at Hazael until the moment became unbearable, and the prophet began to weep.

Hazael asked why. Elisha told him: "Because I know the harm you will do to the Israelites. You will set fire to their fortified cities, kill their young men with the sword, dash their children to the ground, and rip open their pregnant women."

Hazael was stunned. "How could your servant, a mere dog, accomplish such a thing?" Elisha answered: "The Lord has shown me that you will become king of Aram." The next day, Hazael smothered Ben-Hadad with a wet cloth and took the throne.

Elisha's tears are important. God was about to use Hazael as an instrument of judgment against Israel. Decades of apostasy were finally catching up with the nation. But Elisha didn't announce the judgment with satisfaction. He wept. Because that is how God feels about his own judgment. He is just, and justice must come. But he takes no pleasure in it. Even necessary judgment breaks his heart.

The chapter closes with two quick summaries of kings in Judah. Jehoram of Judah married a daughter of Ahab, and Judah began acting like the northern kingdom. His son Ahaziah continued the pattern. The poison of Ahab's family had now infected both kingdoms. Both Jehoram of Israel and Ahaziah of Judah ended up together at Jezreel, recovering from wounds. They had no idea that judgment was already on its way.

WHAT THIS MEANS FOR US

First, God sees more than you see. The servant at Dothan saw an army and panicked. Elisha saw the same army and prayed.

The difference wasn't courage. It was vision. When your problems feel overwhelming, you may be looking at real threats, but you're not seeing the whole picture. God's resources are always greater than your obstacles.

Second, God's timing is precise. The Shunammite woman walked into the king's court at the exact moment Gehazi was telling her story. The lepers walked into the Aramean camp right after God had scattered the army. Neither event was a coincidence. God's timing often doesn't match ours, but it is never late.

Third, unbelief costs more than you think. The officer at the gate mocked Elisha's promise, and it cost him his life. He saw the miracle but couldn't participate in it. The Bible takes unbelief seriously. It's not a minor character flaw. It's a refusal to trust the God who has spoken, and it carries consequences.

Fourth, God's judgment is real but never gleeful. Elisha wept over the destruction Hazael would bring. God doesn't enjoy punishing his people. He is patient, slow to anger, and merciful. But when a nation spends generations running from him, consequences eventually arrive. Even then, God's heart breaks.

TALKING POINTS

1. **Elisha told his servant, "Those who are with us are more than those who are with them."** How does knowing that God's power surrounds you change the way you face situations where you feel outnumbered or outmatched? What does it look like practically to trust in what you can't see?

2. **The four men with skin diseases decided to share the good news of the empty camp instead of keeping it to**

themselves. Why did their conscience bother them? What kind of good news have you received from God that you might be tempted to keep to yourself?

3. **The king of Israel wore sackcloth under his clothes but still wanted to kill Elisha.** What's the difference between going through the motions of repentance and actually trusting God? How can you tell if someone's faith is genuine rather than just a performance?

4. **The Shunammite woman arrived at the king's court at exactly the right moment.** Have you ever experienced timing in your life that felt too perfect to be random? How does recognizing God's hand in those moments strengthen your faith for the future?

5. **Elisha wept when he told Hazael about the destruction he would bring to Israel.** What does it tell us about God's character that his prophet cried over a judgment that was deserved? How should this shape the way we think and talk about God's justice?

An invisible army. An empty camp. A prophet's tears. Through it all, God was proving that he is never absent, never surprised, and never without a plan. But the plan was about to take a violent turn. Israel's sin had been accumulating for generations, and the bill was coming due. A man named Jehu was about to be anointed, and blood was about to flow.

Turn the page.

4

THE BILL COMES DUE

In the movie *Aladdin*, there's a moment when the villain Jafar finally gets what he's been scheming for. He seizes the magic lamp, becomes the most powerful sorcerer in the world, and then wishes to become an all-powerful genie. He gets his wish. But the wish comes with a catch he didn't see coming: every genie is bound to a lamp. Jafar is sucked into a tiny prison of his own making, trapped forever by the very power he craved. The thing he wanted most became the thing that destroyed him.

The house of Ahab had been building toward its own destruction for decades. Ahab and Jezebel introduced Baal worship into Israel, murdered God's prophets, stole land from the innocent, and dragged the nation deeper into idolatry than it had ever been. God had warned them. Elijah had confronted them. Prophets had spoken. But the warnings went unheeded. The family kept grabbing for more power, more control, more of everything except obedience to God.

Now the bill was coming due. What God had promised through Elijah years earlier was about to happen. Every word of it. And the instrument of that judgment was a man named

Jehu, a military commander who drove his chariot like a maniac and wielded a sword without hesitation.

Second Kings 9–10 are among the most violent chapters in the Bible. They are not comfortable to read. But they are honest about what happens when a nation's sin has been accumulating for generations and God finally says, "Enough."

A SECRET ANOINTING

The story begins at Ramoth Gilead, an Israelite military outpost on the border with Aram (Syria). King Joram had been wounded in battle and had gone back to Jezreel to recover, leaving his army officers in charge. Among those officers was a commander named Jehu.

Elisha sent one of the young prophets to Ramoth Gilead with a flask of oil and very specific instructions: Find Jehu. Take him into a private room. Pour the oil on his head. Tell him God has anointed him king over Israel. Then open the door and run. Don't wait around.

The young prophet obeyed. He found Jehu sitting with the other commanders, pulled him into an inner room, poured oil on his head, and delivered God's message: "This is what the Lord, the God of Israel, says: 'I anoint you king over the Lord's people Israel. You are to destroy the house of Ahab your master, and I will avenge the blood of my servants the prophets and the blood of all the Lord's servants shed by Jezebel. The whole house of Ahab will perish.'"

Then the prophet threw open the door and bolted.

The other officers were curious. When Jehu came back out, they pressed him: "What did that madman want?" Jehu tried to brush it off, but they wouldn't let it go. When he told them what had happened, their response was instant. They took their cloaks, spread them on the bare steps, blew a trumpet, and shouted, "Jehu is king!" The revolt had begun.

Notice who set this revolution in motion. Not Jehu. Not the army. God did. Through a young, unnamed prophet with a flask of oil. The word of God was the spark that ignited the fire. Human ambition played its part, certainly. But the catalyst was divine.

THE RIDE TO JEZREEL

Jehu moved fast. He ordered that no one leave Ramoth Gilead to warn anyone in Jezreel. Then he jumped into his chariot and drove toward the king.

A watchman on the tower at Jezreel spotted the approaching company. He sent messengers to find out if this was good news or bad. The first rider galloped out and asked, "Is everything all right?" Jehu told him to fall in behind. The rider didn't come back. A second rider was sent. Same result. Then the watchman delivered his famous observation: "The driving is like that of Jehu son of Nimshi. He drives like a madman."

King Joram, still recovering from his battle wounds, went out to meet Jehu. Ahaziah, king of Judah, who was visiting Joram at the time, went with him. And here the story turns on a bitter piece of irony: they met Jehu at the plot of ground that had once belonged to Naboth the Jezreelite.

Naboth. The man whose vineyard Ahab had coveted. The man Jezebel had framed with false charges and murdered so her husband could seize the land. The man whose innocent blood God had promised to avenge. Years had passed since that crime. Ahab was dead. Jezebel was still alive. The vineyard had been absorbed into royal property. Everyone had moved on. But God hadn't. The land remembered, and so did the God who sees every act of injustice.

Joram called out, "Have you come in peace, Jehu?"

Jehu's answer told Joram everything he needed to know: "How can there be peace as long as the idolatry and witchcraft of your mother Jezebel abound?"

Joram turned to flee. Jehu drew his bow and put an arrow through Joram's heart. The king's body slumped in his chariot. Jehu ordered his officer Bidkar to throw the body onto Naboth's field, recalling the prophecy God had spoken over Ahab in that very place: "I will pay you back on this plot of ground."

Ahaziah, the king of Judah, tried to escape but was also struck down. He had tied himself to the house of Ahab through marriage and alliance, and now he was caught up in the judgment meant for Ahab's family. His choice of friends proved fatal.

THE QUEEN IN THE WINDOW

Jehu entered Jezreel. By now, Jezebel had heard what happened. She knew Jehu was coming for her.

What she did next tells you everything about who she was. She put on eye makeup. She arranged her hair. She sat in a window and waited.

This was not a woman trying to seduce her way out of danger. This was defiance. Jezebel was going out on her own terms. When Jehu rode through the gate, she called down to him with cutting sarcasm: "Have you come in peace, you Zimri, you murderer of your master?" The reference to Zimri was a taunt. Zimri was a previous king of Israel who had assassinated his way to the throne and lasted only seven days before killing himself. Jezebel was telling Jehu that his revolution would fail just as badly.

She was wrong.

Jehu looked up at the window and shouted, "Who is on my side? Who?" Two or three palace servants leaned out. Jehu ordered them to throw her down. They did. Jezebel fell from the window. Some of her blood spattered on the wall and on the horses. Jehu drove his chariot over her body and went inside to eat.

After his meal, he ordered that she be buried. She was, after all, a king's daughter. But when the servants went out to get her, they found almost nothing left. Dogs had eaten her remains. Only her skull, her feet, and the palms of her hands were left.

When they reported this to Jehu, he quoted Elijah's prophecy: "This is the word of the Lord that he spoke through his servant Elijah: On the plot of ground at Jezreel dogs will devour Jezebel's flesh. Her body will be like refuse on the ground, so that no one will be able to say, 'Here is Jezebel's grave.'"

Every word came true. The queen who had terrorized God's prophets for years, who had introduced Baal worship and murdered the innocent, who had manipulated courts and corrupted kings, who had thought herself untouchable, was reduced to scraps on the ground. It was horrifying. It was meant to be. This is what the Bible looks like when it refuses to sanitize the consequences of evil. Jezebel's end was exactly what God had said would happen, spoken through Elijah years earlier, fulfilled down to the smallest detail.

SEVENTY HEADS AND A TEMPLE FULL OF WORSHIPERS

Chapter 10 continues the bloodshed. Ahab had seventy descendants living in Samaria under the care of the city's leading men. Jehu sent letters to these leaders, essentially daring them to pick one of Ahab's sons and fight for the old dynasty. They refused. They were too afraid. So Jehu sent a second letter: prove your loyalty by sending me the heads of Ahab's descendants.

The next morning, seventy heads arrived in baskets at Jezreel. Jehu had them stacked in two piles at the city gate, then addressed the people: "You are fair judges. I conspired against my master and killed him. But who killed all these? Know then that not a word the Lord has spoken against the house of Ahab will fail. The Lord has done what he announced through his servant Elijah."

This is the theological center of the passage. Jehu wasn't claiming innocence. He was making a point about God's word. Everything that was happening, as terrible as it was, had been predicted. God had announced judgment against Ahab's house through Elijah, and every detail was being fulfilled. The piles of severed heads were gruesome evidence that when God speaks, it happens.

On his way to Samaria, Jehu also killed forty-two relatives of Ahaziah, king of Judah. They had the misfortune of being connected to the house of Ahab by marriage, and they stumbled into Jehu's path at the worst possible moment.

Then came the Baal worshipers. Jehu announced that he intended to serve Baal even more enthusiastically than Ahab had. He called a massive assembly of every prophet, priest, and servant of Baal in Israel. He made sure they all came. He distributed special robes to identify them. He personally offered sacrifices in Baal's temple.

It was all a trap. Once the sacrifice was complete, Jehu stationed eighty armed men outside and gave the order: "Go in and kill them. Let no one escape." The soldiers obeyed. They slaughtered every Baal worshiper in the building, demolished the sacred stone of Baal, tore down the temple, and turned the site into a latrine.

One verse captures the result: "So Jehu destroyed Baal worship in Israel."

NOT FAR ENOUGH

If the story ended there, Jehu might look like a hero. But the writer of 2 Kings refuses to let us see it that way. Immediately after recording Jehu's destruction of Baal worship, the text delivers a devastating qualification. "However, he did not turn away from the sins of Jeroboam son of Nebat, which he had caused Israel to commit. He did not turn away from the golden calves that were in Bethel and Dan."

Jehu wiped out Baal but kept the golden calves. He eliminated the most extreme form of idolatry but clung to the older, more "respectable" counterfeit religion that Jeroboam had established when the kingdom first split. He went far enough to consolidate his political power but not far enough to actually obey God from the heart. It is one of the saddest patterns in

Scripture: a leader who does something genuinely courageous for God but stops short of full surrender. The revolution looked impressive from the outside. On the inside, it was hollow.

God acknowledged what Jehu had done right. He promised Jehu's descendants would sit on the throne for four generations, the longest dynasty in the history of the northern kingdom. But it was limited blessing for limited obedience. And the very next verses record the consequences of Jehu's half-hearted faithfulness: "In those days the Lord began to reduce the size of Israel. Hazael overpowered the Israelites throughout their territory." The land east of the Jordan was stripped away.

Jehu served as God's instrument of judgment against the house of Ahab. Then God raised up Hazael as an instrument of judgment against Jehu. One flawed tool replaced by another. This is the sobering pattern of history when nations refuse to turn fully to God. The revolution always promises more than it delivers, because revolutions change governments but not hearts.

WHAT THIS MEANS FOR US

First, God keeps his word, even when it takes years. The prophecies against the house of Ahab were spoken during Elijah's ministry, years before Jehu ever picked up a sword. It looked like those words might never be fulfilled. But God was patient, not absent. When the time came, every single detail happened exactly as he said. God's promises work the same way. If he has spoken it, you can count on it, no matter how long it takes.

Second, sin's consequences eventually arrive. The house of Ahab accumulated wickedness for decades. For a while, it looked like they were getting away with it. They weren't. God gave warning after warning, chance after chance. But when the bill finally came due, it came all at once. This should make us take sin seriously. The fact that consequences haven't shown up yet doesn't mean they won't.

Third, being used by God is not the same as being right with God. Jehu carried out God's will against Ahab's house. God himself acknowledged it. But Jehu's heart was never fully surrendered to God. He used God's mission for his own political advantage and stopped obeying the moment it stopped benefiting him. You can do impressive things in God's name and still not belong to him. What matters is not just what you do for God but whether your heart is actually his.

Fourth, halfway obedience is still disobedience. Jehu destroyed Baal but kept the golden calves. He did the dramatic, visible, publicly impressive act of reform but left the quieter, deeper sin untouched. God calls us to more than dramatic gestures. He wants the hidden idols too. The ones nobody else can see. The ones that are harder to give up because they've been there so long they feel normal.

TALKING POINTS

1. **Jezebel faced death with defiance and sarcasm rather than repentance.** Why do you think some people resist God even when the consequences of their choices are staring them in the face? What makes repentance so hard for some people?

2. **Joram met Jehu on the very plot of ground that had belonged to Naboth.** What does this detail tell us about how God views injustice? Does knowing that God remembers the

wrongs done to innocent people give you comfort or make you uncomfortable? Why?

3. **Jehu told the people of Israel that everything happening was the fulfillment of God's word through Elijah.** Why is the fulfillment of God's word such an important theme in 1 and 2 Kings? How does seeing God keep his promises in the past help you trust him with the future?

4. **Jehu destroyed Baal worship but kept the golden calves.** What is the difference between doing something dramatic for God and truly obeying him from the heart? Are there areas in your life where you might be giving God partial obedience while holding something back?

5. **These chapters are extremely violent, and the Bible doesn't try to make them comfortable.** Why do you think God allowed the judgment against Ahab's house to be carried out in such a brutal way? How do you reconcile God's love with his justice?

The house of Ahab was gone. Baal worship was destroyed. But the deeper rot in Israel remained. Jehu had changed the government, but he hadn't changed the nation's heart. And in the shadows, a woman from Ahab's own family was about to seize power in Judah and nearly wipe out the line of David forever.

Turn the page.

5

THE BABY WHO SAVED THE LINE

In *Sleeping Beauty*, the kingdom throws a celebration for the birth of a princess. Everyone is invited. Gifts are given. The future looks bright. Then Maleficent shows up. Furious at being overlooked, she curses the child: before her sixteenth birthday, Aurora will prick her finger on a spinning wheel and die. The entire kingdom panics. The king orders every spinning wheel in the land burned. Three good fairies smuggle the baby away to a cottage in the woods, where she grows up hidden, her true identity a secret even from herself. For sixteen years, the most important person in the kingdom lives in obscurity, and the villain has no idea she's still alive.

Second Kings 11 is that story, except it's real, and the stakes are infinitely higher. This isn't about a sleeping princess. It's about the survival of God's promise. The entire line of David, the royal family through which God had promised to bring his kingdom and ultimately the Messiah, is about to be wiped off the face of the earth by a woman who makes Maleficent look restrained. One baby is all that stands between God's covenant and total extinction.

And nobody knows he's alive.

THE QUEEN WHO KILLED HER OWN FAMILY

When Jehu's revolution swept through Israel and killed King Ahaziah of Judah (who had been visiting at the wrong time), the news traveled south fast. Athaliah, Ahaziah's mother, heard that her son was dead.

You need to understand who Athaliah was. She was the daughter of Ahab and Jezebel, the infamous royal couple of the northern kingdom. She had married into Judah's royal family as part of a political alliance, bringing the poison of Baal worship south with her. Her husband Jehoram had killed all his own brothers when he took the throne. Philistines and Arabs had carried off or killed most of Jehoram's sons. Then Jehu killed Ahaziah along with forty-two of Judah's royal relatives. The Davidic family tree had already been hacked nearly to the stump.

And now Athaliah finished the job. When she learned her son was dead, "she proceeded to destroy the whole royal family." Her own grandchildren. The babies and boys who carried the blood of David in their veins. She killed them all to seize the throne for herself.

Think about what that means in the bigger story. God had promised David that his line would endure forever. That promise was the backbone of Israel's hope. One day, a descendant of David would sit on an eternal throne. Every prophet pointed toward it. Every psalm celebrated it. And now, in a single bloody morning, a power-hungry grandmother was trying to make that promise impossible.

This is the pattern. Wherever God makes a promise, an enemy rises to destroy it. Pharaoh tried to kill the Hebrew babies. Herod would later try to kill the baby Jesus. And here, Athaliah tried to wipe out the line of David. The darkness always aims at the promise.

ONE BABY, ONE AUNT, ONE HIDING PLACE

But Athaliah missed one. Jehosheba, the sister of the dead king Ahaziah, grabbed the youngest prince before the killers could reach him. His name was Joash, and he was still an infant. Jehosheba snatched him and his nurse out of the room where the royal children were being slaughtered and hid them in a storage room in the temple complex. From there, she kept the boy hidden inside the temple of the Lord for six years while Athaliah ruled the land.

Six years. Think about that. For six years, the rightful king of Judah lived in secret, tucked away in the one place Athaliah apparently never thought to look. The true king was growing up in God's house while the false queen sat on the throne. The woman who worshiped Baal never imagined that the heir of David was being raised right under her nose, inside the very temple of the God she despised.

Jehosheba is one of the most important people in the Bible that almost nobody talks about. She wasn't a prophet or a warrior. She was a woman who saw an emergency, acted with courage, and kept a secret for six years. According to 2 Chronicles, she was married to Jehoiada the priest, which means she had connections inside the temple. That mattered. But connections alone don't explain what she did. She walked into a massacre and walked out with a baby. Without her, the line of David would have ended. Without her, there would have been no fulfillment of God's promise. Without her, humanly speaking, there would have been no Jesus.

And yet God didn't use a spectacular miracle to save the line of David. No angel appeared. No fire fell from heaven. God used one brave woman who grabbed a baby and hid him in a closet. That's how God works. He plants his servants in the right place at the right time, and then the ordinary courage of ordinary people becomes the hinge on which history turns.

THE SEVENTH YEAR

When Joash turned seven, the priest Jehoiada decided it was time. Jehoiada was married to Jehosheba, which means he had been in on the secret from the beginning. For six years he had watched and waited. Now he moved.

Jehoiada called a secret meeting with the commanders of the royal guard. He showed them the king's son. The boy was alive. The line of David was intact. The commanders swore an oath of loyalty.

Then Jehoiada laid out a careful plan. On the Sabbath, when the guard rotations were changing, he positioned soldiers at every key point around the temple. Armed men surrounded the young prince. The spears and shields that had belonged to King David himself, stored in the temple for generations, were handed to the commanders. Everything was in place.

Jehoiada brought Joash out. He placed the crown on his head. He gave him a copy of God's covenant law, the document that was supposed to guide every king of Judah, reminding him that he ruled under God's authority, not his own. Then Jehoiada anointed him, the people clapped their hands, and the shout went up: "Long live the king!"

It was a moment that almost didn't happen. A crown on the head of a seven-year-old boy who had spent his entire life hiding in a temple. The covenant had survived by the thinnest of margins.

TREASON! TREASON!

Athaliah heard the noise. The cheering and the trumpet blasts carried from the temple to the palace, and she came running. When she reached the temple and saw what was happening, her reaction tells you everything. There was the boy, standing by the pillar, wearing the crown, surrounded by guards and officers and people celebrating. Athaliah tore her robes and screamed: "Treason! Treason!"

The word is almost funny coming from her. She had murdered her own grandchildren to steal the throne. She had no legitimate claim to power. She was the treasonous one. But that is how usurpers think. They sit on stolen thrones long enough that they start believing they belong there, and anyone who challenges them becomes the criminal.

Jehoiada gave the order: take her out of the temple and execute anyone who follows her. The soldiers seized Athaliah, led her away through the horse gate near the palace, and killed her there.

The false queen was dead. The true king was on the throne. And the first thing Jehoiada did was lead the entire nation in renewing their covenant with God.

COVENANT AND DEMOLITION

What happened next is recorded in a single verse, but it might be the most important moment in the chapter. Jehoiada made a covenant between the Lord and the king and the people, that they would be the Lord's people. Then he made a separate covenant between the king and the people, defining the king's responsibilities to the nation.

This was not a new agreement. It was a renewal of the old one, the covenant God had made with Israel at Sinai. After years of Baal worship under Athaliah, after the corruption that Ahab's daughter had brought south from Israel, Judah was recommitting itself to the God who had chosen them. It was a fresh start.

And fresh starts require cleanup. The people marched to the temple of Baal that Athaliah had built in Jerusalem and tore it apart. They smashed the altars. They shattered the idols. They killed Mattan, the priest of Baal. Covenant renewal and idol destruction went hand in hand. You couldn't have one without the other. If you were going to be the Lord's people, you had to get rid of everything that competed with him.

Then Jehoiada stationed guards at the temple of the Lord and led Joash in a procession from the temple to the palace, where the boy sat on the royal throne. The city was quiet. The text says, "All the people of the land rejoiced, and the city was calm, because Athaliah had been slain."

Peace. After six years of illegitimate rule, after the blood of David's family staining the ground, after the nation bowing to Baal in God's own capital city, there was peace. Not because the problems were over, but because the rightful king was back where he belonged.

A GOOD START, A DISAPPOINTING FINISH

Chapter 12 tells the rest of Joash's story, and it reads like a slow deflation. Joash reigned for forty years. He did what was right in the eyes of the Lord, the text says, all the years Jehoiada the priest instructed him. That qualifier is important. As long as the priest was guiding him, Joash stayed on track.

His main project was repairing the temple. The building had fallen into serious disrepair during the years of Baal worship under Athaliah, and Joash ordered the priests to use the regular offerings that came in to fund the necessary repairs. But the priests dragged their feet. Year after year, the money came in and nothing happened. By Joash's twenty-third year on the throne, not a single repair had been made. The priests had been collecting the money but spending it on their own needs instead of the building. It wasn't necessarily theft in the dramatic sense. They just never got around to doing what the king had told them to do. The money quietly disappeared into their own pockets while the temple crumbled.

Joash confronted them and set up a new system. A chest with a hole in the lid was placed beside the altar. When the chest filled up, the royal secretary and the high priest would count the money together and pay the workers directly. The system worked. The temple was repaired. Carpenters, builders, masons, and stonecutters did the work, and the supervisors handled the funds with complete honesty.

But then Hazael, king of Aram, attacked. He captured the

city of Gath and turned toward Jerusalem. And Joash, rather than trusting God, emptied the temple. He took all the sacred objects and all the gold from both the temple treasuries and the palace and sent them to Hazael as a bribe to go away. It worked. Hazael withdrew. But the cost was devastating. The very temple Joash had spent years repairing, he now stripped bare to buy off a foreign king.

The story ends with Joash's own officials conspiring against him and assassinating him. The king who had been saved as an infant, crowned as a child, and guided by a faithful priest for decades finished his reign in disappointment and violence. His son Amaziah took the throne. The line of David continued, but the pattern was becoming painfully familiar: good beginnings followed by bad endings.

WHAT THIS MEANS FOR US

First, God's promises survive the worst attacks. Athaliah murdered nearly every member of the royal family, and God's promise to David still held. The enemy threw everything at the covenant, and one baby in a storage room was enough to preserve it. Whatever threatens God's purposes in your life is not stronger than his commitment to keep his word.

Second, God uses ordinary people in extraordinary moments. Jehosheba wasn't a prophet or a general. She was an aunt who grabbed a baby. But her courage preserved the line that would produce Jesus. You don't have to be famous or powerful to play a crucial role in what God is doing. You just have to be faithful when the moment comes.

Third, renewal requires removal. The covenant ceremony

in chapter 11 was immediately followed by the destruction of Baal's temple. You can't recommit your life to God while holding on to the things that pull you away from him. Real repentance isn't just saying yes to God. It's saying no to everything that competes with him.

Fourth, good beginnings don't guarantee good endings. Joash started well. He had the best mentor imaginable in Jehoiada. But when the priest's influence faded and pressure mounted, Joash caved. The lesson isn't that faithfulness is impossible. The lesson is that faithfulness requires daily dependence on God, not just a strong start. What you do in the middle and at the end matters just as much as how you begin.

TALKING POINTS

1. **Athaliah tried to destroy the entire royal family to seize power for herself.** Why do you think enemies of God so often target the things God has promised to protect? How does seeing God preserve his promises in the past give you confidence for the future?

2. **Jehosheba risked her life to save one baby.** What does her story teach you about the value of doing the right thing even when it's dangerous and no one is watching? Can you think of a time when one person's quiet courage made a huge difference?

3. **For six years, the true king was hidden in the temple while a false queen ruled the land.** How does this picture of a hidden king help you understand what it means to trust God when the wrong people seem to be in charge? How does this point forward to Jesus?

4. Joash did what was right "all the years Jehoiada the priest instructed him." What does that tell us about the importance of having wise, godly people in our lives? Who are the people who help keep you on track with God, and how can you stay connected to them?

5. **Joash spent years repairing the temple, then emptied it to pay off a foreign king.** What does his story teach us about the danger of abandoning our convictions when we're under pressure? How can we guard against the pattern of starting well but finishing poorly?

The line of David had survived its closest brush with extinction. A baby hidden in a temple, a brave aunt, a faithful priest, and a God who refuses to let his promises die. But the story of Judah's kings was only half told, and the story of Israel's kings was about to take its final, devastating turn.

Turn the page.

6

THE KINGDOM THAT WOULDN'T LISTEN

In *Up*, Carl Fredricksen spends his whole life dreaming about one adventure: flying his house to Paradise Falls in South America. He and his wife Ellie had planned the trip since childhood, but life kept getting in the way. A flat tire. A broken leg. A tree falling on the roof. Every time they saved up enough money, something happened and the jar got emptied again. Then Ellie died, and Carl was alone in a house full of memories and a dream that never came true.

What makes *Up* so heartbreaking is not one single disaster. It's the slow accumulation. The repeated cycle of hope and disappointment. You watch Carl and Ellie's life speed by in a montage, and by the end of it you feel the weight of all those years pressing down on one old man sitting in an empty room.

Second Kings 13–17 feels like that montage. Five chapters cover roughly 150 years, and during those years the northern kingdom of Israel slides from sickness to ruin. King follows king. Conspiracies pile up. Prophets warn. Nobody listens. There are brief moments of hope, flashes of mercy where God pulls Israel back from the edge. But every time, the nation returns to the same sins that are killing it. And by the end of chapter 17, the kingdom is gone. Erased from the map. Carried off to Assyria, never to return.

This is the story of a nation that had every chance to survive and chose not to.

A DYING PROPHET AND A HALFHEARTED KING

Chapter 13 opens during the reign of Jehoahaz, son of Jehu. Israel was being crushed by Hazael, king of Aram, just as Elisha had predicted through his tears back in chapter 8. Hazael squeezed Israel so hard that Jehoahaz's army was reduced to almost nothing: fifty horsemen, ten chariots, and ten thousand foot soldiers. That's it. A nation brought to its knees.

In his desperation, Jehoahaz did something surprising: he prayed. He pleaded with God for help. And God listened. Not because Jehoahaz deserved it. Not because he had turned away from the golden calves. He hadn't. God listened because he saw how badly the Arameans were oppressing his people. The text reaches all the way back to the book of Exodus for its language: God "saw the oppression of Israel." The same God who saw Hebrew slaves suffering under Pharaoh's whip saw Israelites suffering under Hazael's sword. His compassion hadn't changed, even though his people had.

God gave Israel a deliverer, and for a while things got better. But the very next verse delivers the verdict: "Nevertheless, they did not turn away from the sins of the house of Jeroboam." Mercy came, and gratitude didn't follow. God rescued them, and they went right back to the golden calves.

Then Elisha got sick. This was the final illness, the one that would kill him. King Jehoash (son of Jehoahaz) came to visit the dying prophet and wept over him, using the same words Elisha himself had cried when Elijah was taken: "My father! My father! The chariots and horsemen of Israel!" He understood that losing Elisha meant losing Israel's greatest defense.

Elisha had one last message. He told the king to take a bow and arrows, open the east window, and shoot. As the king drew the bow, Elisha placed his own hands over the king's hands. The arrow flew. "The arrow of the Lord's victory over Aram!" Elisha declared. Then he told Jehoash to take the remaining arrows and strike the ground.

The king struck three times and stopped.

Elisha was furious. "You should have struck five or six times! Then you would have completely destroyed Aram. But now you will defeat them only three times." God had offered a blank check of victory, and the king cashed only half of it. The promise didn't stir him enough to grab it with everything he had. He was content with partial victory when total victory was on the table. It is a warning to anyone who hears God's promises and responds with a shrug instead of a shout.

Elisha died. But the story of his power didn't end with his burial. Some time later, a group of Israelites were burying a man when they spotted a band of raiders. In a panic, they threw the body into Elisha's tomb. When the corpse touched Elisha's bones, the man came back to life and stood on his feet.

It's a strange story. But the point is clear: the power of God that had worked through Elisha was not extinguished by death. Even in the grave, God's prophet testified that death does not have the final word. For a nation spiraling toward its own grave, that was a message worth hearing.

OCTOBER IN ISRAEL

If you've ever lived somewhere with real seasons, you know that October is the last beautiful month before everything turns brown and cold. The leaves are brilliant, the air is perfect, and for a few weeks it feels like the good weather might last forever. It never does. Winter always comes.

What follows in chapter 14 was a brief and deceptive golden age. Jeroboam II, the great-grandson of Jehu, took the throne of Israel and reigned for forty-one years. He was the most militarily successful king Israel had seen in generations. He restored Israel's borders to their widest extent, recovering territory that had been lost to Aram for decades. The economy boomed. The nation expanded. By every visible measure, Israel was thriving.

But the writer of 2 Kings barely gives Jeroboam II the time of day. His entire reign gets seven verses. And the key verse isn't about Jeroboam's achievements. It's about why God allowed those achievements: "The Lord had seen how bitterly everyone in Israel was suffering. There was no one to help them. And since the Lord had not said he would blot out the name of Israel from under heaven, he saved them by the hand of Jeroboam."

Read that carefully. God didn't bless Israel because Jeroboam was righteous. The text says explicitly that Jeroboam "did evil in the eyes of the Lord" and never departed from Jeroboam son of Nebat's sins. God blessed Israel because he pitied them. Prosperity was a sign of God's compassion, not his approval. And that distinction matters enormously. It is dangerously easy to look at a thriving nation, a growing church, or a comfortable life and assume God must be pleased with the way things are going. Sometimes he's just being patient.

The prophets Amos and Hosea preached during Jeroboam II's reign, and their message was the opposite of what the national mood suggested. While Israel celebrated its wealth and success, these prophets warned that judgment was right around the corner. The rich were exploiting the poor. Worship had become a hollow performance. Justice was for sale. And underneath all the prosperity, the rot was spreading.

October doesn't last.

FIVE KINGS AND A COUNTDOWN TO ZERO

After Jeroboam II died, the bottom fell out. Chapter 15 fast-forwards through the last three decades of Israel's existence at dizzying speed. Five kings in roughly twenty years. Four of them were assassinated. One lasted only a single month on the throne.

Zechariah, Jeroboam's son, reigned six months before Shallum murdered him in public. With his death, the dynasty God had promised Jehu came to its end, exactly as God had said: four generations, no more. Shallum lasted one month before Menahem killed him. Menahem held power for ten years through sheer brutality, but the real story of his reign is a single verse: Tiglath-Pileser III of Assyria showed up, and Menahem paid him a thousand talents of silver to prop up his throne. The shadow of Assyria was falling over Israel.

Menahem's son Pekahiah lasted two years before his own officer, Pekah, assassinated him. Pekah tried to resist Assyria by forming an alliance with Aram, but Tiglath-Pileser invaded anyway, conquered the northern and eastern territories, and deported the population. Israel shrank to a tiny rump state centered on Samaria. Then Hoshea assassinated Pekah and became the last king Israel would ever have.

While all this chaos consumed the north, Judah's situation was deteriorating too. King Ahaz brought the worst of pagan religion into Jerusalem. He sacrificed his own son in the fire. He copied a pagan altar he saw in Damascus and had it installed in the Lord's temple. He stripped the temple of its bronze furnishings. When threatened by Aram and Israel, he refused to trust God and instead sold himself to Assyria as a vassal, declaring to the Assyrian king: "I am your servant and your son." That title belonged to God alone. Ahaz was trading his covenant birthright for a political alliance.

The darkness was thickening in both kingdoms.

THE END OF ISRAEL

Chapter 17 is the funeral. Hoshea, the last king, tried to play a double game. He stopped paying tribute to Assyria and secretly negotiated with Egypt for help. It was a desperate gamble, and it failed spectacularly. Assyria found out. Shalmaneser V arrested Hoshea, invaded Israel, and besieged Samaria. For three years the city held out behind its walls while its people slowly starved. Then the walls fell. The people were deported to cities in Assyria and Media, scattered across a foreign empire, absorbed into populations that did not know their God or their story. The kingdom of Israel was finished.

And then the writer pauses. He puts down the history and picks up a sermon. For eleven straight verses, he explains why this happened. It is the longest theological reflection in the entire book of Kings, and it is devastating.

"All this took place because the Israelites had sinned against the Lord their God, who had brought them up out of Egypt." That's where it starts. Everything traces back to the exodus. God had rescued them. He had brought them out of slavery, carried them through the wilderness, planted them in a land of their own. And they turned around and worshiped other gods.

The writer piles up the charges like a prosecutor building a case. They built high places in every town. They set up sacred stones and poles on every hill. They burned offerings at the pagan shrines. They worshiped idols, the very thing God had told them never to do. They rejected God's statutes and his covenant. They followed worthless idols and became worthless themselves. They sacrificed their own children in the fire. They practiced divination and sorcery. They sold themselves to do evil.

And through it all, God warned them. "The Lord warned Israel and Judah through all his prophets and seers: 'Turn from your evil ways.'" Prophet after prophet, generation after generation, God sent messengers. But "they would not listen and were as stiff-necked as their ancestors, who did not trust in the Lord their God."

Three times the writer repeats the final verdict in slightly different words: God removed Israel from his presence. God cast them from his presence. God banished them from his sight. It is the most terrible sentence in the Old Testament. Not military defeat. Not economic collapse. Removal from the presence of God.

The Assyrians repopulated the land with foreigners who brought their own gods. When lions began attacking the settlers, they sent for a priest from the exiled Israelites to teach them how to worship "the god of the land." But what they practiced was a religious buffet. The writer's verdict is blunt: "They worshiped the Lord, but they also served their own idols." To which he adds, with unmistakable clarity: "They did not worship the Lord."

You can't worship the Lord and serve idols. You can't hedge your bets with one foot in the temple and one foot at a pagan shrine. God demands all or nothing. That was the lesson Israel refused to learn for over two hundred years. And it cost them everything.

WHAT THIS MEANS FOR US

First, God's patience has limits. God warned Israel for over two centuries. He sent prophets. He allowed suffering to get their attention. He gave them periods of relief and prosperity. He did everything short of overriding their free will. But when a nation (or a person) refuses to listen long enough, the consequences finally arrive. God's patience is real and generous, but it is not the same as permission.

Second, prosperity is not proof of God's approval. Jeroboam II's Israel was wealthy, powerful, and expanding. It was also spiritually bankrupt. God blessed them out of pity, not pleasure. If your life is going well, don't automatically assume God is pleased with everything in it. Sometimes his kindness is a last invitation to change before things get harder.

Third, we become like what we worship. The writer says Israel "followed worthless idols and became worthless." Whatever you give your deepest loyalty to will shape who you become. If you chase things that have no lasting value, you will find your own life emptying out. But the reverse is also true: if you worship the God who is real and good, his character will begin to mark yours.

Fourth, the sin you refuse to deal with is the sin that destroys you. From its first king to its last, Israel clung to Jeroboam's golden calves. Over two hundred years, not a single king turned away from them. That one tolerated sin outlasted every dynasty, survived every crisis, and finally dragged the nation into exile. The habits you refuse to address today don't go away on their own. They grow roots.

TALKING POINTS

1. **God rescued Israel from Aramean oppression even though they hadn't repented.** Why do you think God sometimes shows mercy to people who don't deserve it? What should our response be when God is kind to us even when we know we've been unfaithful?

2. **Elisha was angry that King Jehoash only struck the ground three times.** What does that tell us about how God wants us to respond to his promises? Is there an area in your life where you might be settling for less than what God is offering?

3. **Israel experienced a golden age under Jeroboam II while ignoring God.** Why is it dangerous to assume that success and comfort mean God is happy with us? How can we stay spiritually alert during good times?

4. **The writer of 2 Kings says God warned Israel "through all his prophets and seers," but the people "would not lis-**

ten." What are some ways God warns people today? Why do you think it's so hard for us to hear and respond to correction?

5. **Chapter 17 says Israel "followed worthless idols and became worthless."** What does it mean to become like what you worship? What are some "idols" in today's culture that shape people in harmful ways without them even realizing it?

Israel was gone. The ten northern tribes had been scattered across the Assyrian empire, and foreigners had taken their place in the land. But Judah still stood. The line of David still held. And in Jerusalem, a new king was about to take the throne who would do something none of his recent predecessors had done: he would actually trust God. His name was Hezekiah, and his story is one of the brightest lights in the entire Old Testament.

Turn the page.

7

THE KING WHO TRUSTED

In *Beauty and the Beast*, there is a moment near the end when all seems lost. The Beast has been stabbed. Belle is weeping over his body. The last petal falls from the enchanted rose, and one by one the servants in the castle turn permanently into household objects. The curse has won. The story is over.

And then it isn't. Belle whispers that she loves him, and light pours from the sky. The Beast rises. The curse breaks. The servants come back to life. The castle is restored. Everything that looked dead and finished moments ago is suddenly, impossibly, alive again.

Second Kings 18–20 is the story of a king who looked at impossible odds and chose to trust God anyway. His name was Hezekiah, and the writer of Kings gives him the highest compliment any king of Judah ever received: he trusted in the Lord, the God of Israel, and there was no one like him among all the kings of Judah, either before him or after him.

That's extraordinary praise. But Hezekiah's story isn't a fairy tale. It's the story of genuine faith tested by a terrifying enemy, a fatal illness, and a moment of foolishness that would cast a long shadow over everything he'd built. Even the best king in Judah's history was not the king God's people were ultimately waiting for.

A NEW DAVID

After the spiritual wasteland of Ahaz's reign, Hezekiah's arrival on the throne must have felt like the first warm day after a brutal winter. The text says he did what was right in the eyes of the Lord, "just as his father David had done." No qualifications. No "but he didn't quite go far enough." For the first time since David himself, a king of Judah received an unqualified endorsement.

And Hezekiah earned it. He removed the high places that even the "good" kings before him had left standing. He smashed the sacred stones. He cut down the wooden poles used in pagan worship. He even destroyed the bronze serpent that Moses had made in the wilderness centuries earlier, because the people had started burning incense to it. A relic from Moses, with genuine historical significance, and Hezekiah ground it to powder. Anything that competed with God had to go.

The writer sums up Hezekiah's character in a single sentence: "He trusted in the Lord, the God of Israel." Then he unpacks what that trust looked like in practice: Hezekiah held fast to the Lord. He did not stop following him. He kept the commands God had given through Moses. And because of that trust, God was with him, and he was successful in everything he undertook. He even rebelled against the king of Assyria and refused to serve him.

That last detail is not a throwaway line. Refusing to submit to Assyria was the boldest political decision a small kingdom could make. Assyria had already swallowed the northern kingdom whole. Every nation in the region either paid tribute or was destroyed. Hezekiah looked at the most powerful empire on earth and said no.

THE ASSYRIAN AT THE GATE

The consequences came in 701 BC. Sennacherib, king of Assyria, invaded Judah and captured every fortified city except Jerusalem. The text says it plainly and doesn't soften the blow. Hezekiah's faith did not prevent Assyria from devastating his country.

In a moment of panic, Hezekiah tried to buy Sennacherib off. He sent a message saying, "I have done wrong. Withdraw from me, and I will pay whatever you demand." Sennacherib demanded an enormous sum. Hezekiah stripped the temple and the palace treasuries, even peeling the gold off the temple doors, and sent it all to the Assyrian king.

It didn't work. Sennacherib took the money and sent his army to Jerusalem anyway. He stationed his officers outside the city walls with a massive force, and his chief spokesman, the Rabshakeh, delivered a speech designed to break Jerusalem's will to resist.

The Rabshakeh's argument was brilliant and terrifying. He attacked every possible source of hope the people of Jerusalem might cling to. Egypt? A broken reed that will stab your hand if you lean on it. Your own military? You couldn't even handle two thousand horses if we gave them to you. Your God? He's the one whose high places and altars Hezekiah tore down. Why would he help you now?

That last point was a clever political move. The Rabshakeh knew that not everyone in Judah had been thrilled about Hezekiah's reforms. Some people liked their high places. By suggesting that Hezekiah had offended his own God, the Assyrian was trying to turn the people against their king.

Then the Rabshakeh made his boldest claim: "The Lord himself told me to march against this country and destroy it." He was lying. But it was effective propaganda.

Hezekiah's officials begged the Rabshakeh to speak in Aramaic, the diplomatic language, rather than in the local dialect everyone could understand. They didn't want the soldiers on the wall to hear. The Rabshakeh refused. His whole purpose was to terrify the common people. He shouted up at the men on the wall, offering them a deal: surrender, and you'll eat from your own vines and drink from your own wells. Resist, and you'll starve.

Then came his final argument, the one he thought was unanswerable: "Has the god of any nation ever delivered his land from the hand of the king of Assyria? Where are the gods of Hamath and Arpad? Where are the gods of Sepharvaim? Did they deliver Samaria? Who among all the gods of these countries has been able to save his land from me? How then can the Lord deliver Jerusalem from my hand?"

It was a powerful argument. And it was also the dumbest thing he ever said. Because every god on that list was a piece of wood or stone. The Rabshakeh assumed that the God of Israel was just another local deity who could be swept aside like all the others. He had no idea who he was talking about.

The people on the wall said nothing. Hezekiah had ordered

them not to respond. His officials went back and reported everything to the king with their clothes torn in grief. It was the darkest day Jerusalem had seen in a generation.

THE PRAYER THAT CHANGED EVERYTHING

Hezekiah tore his own clothes, put on sackcloth, and went to the temple. He also sent messengers to the prophet Isaiah, confessing that this was "a day of distress and punishment" and asking Isaiah to pray.

Isaiah's response was immediate and specific: "Don't be afraid of what you have heard. God is going to put a spirit in Sennacherib so that he hears a rumor and returns to his own land. And there he will fall by the sword."

But Sennacherib wasn't finished. He sent another message directly to Hezekiah, pressing the same argument: don't let your God deceive you. No god has ever stopped Assyria. You won't be the exception.

Hezekiah took the letter, went into the temple, and spread it out before the Lord. Then he prayed one of the most important prayers in the Old Testament.

He began by naming who God is: "Lord, God of Israel, enthroned between the cherubim, you alone are God over all the kingdoms of the earth. You have made heaven and earth." In the middle of a crisis, Hezekiah started by reminding himself of the truth about God. He isn't one deity among many. He made everything. He rules everything.

Then Hezekiah made his case: "It is true, Lord, that the Assyrian kings have destroyed these nations and their lands. They have thrown their gods into the fire and destroyed them, because they were not gods at all but only wood and stone." He conceded the Rabshakeh's point. Yes, Assyria had crushed every nation in its path. But none of those nations had a real God defending them. The God of Israel was something Assyria had never encountered before.

Finally, the petition: "Now, Lord our God, deliver us from his hand, so that all the kingdoms of the earth may know that you alone, Lord, are God."

Notice what drove Hezekiah's prayer. Not just survival. Not just national pride. He wanted the whole world to know who God was. When the passion behind our prayers is God's glory rather than our comfort, something shifts.

THE TERROR OF THE NIGHT

Isaiah sent Hezekiah a message from God. It was long, detailed, and devastating for Assyria. God mocked Sennacherib's arrogance through the prophet's words. The Assyrian king boasted of conquering mountains and drying up rivers. God's response was essentially: "Did you think you did all that on your own? I planned it long ago. I ordained it in ancient times. You were my instrument, and you didn't even know it."

Then came the promise. Sennacherib would not enter Jerusalem. He would not shoot a single arrow at it. He would not build a siege ramp against it. He would go home the way he came. God would defend the city for his own sake and for the sake of his promise to David.

That night, the angel of the Lord went through the Assyrian camp. When morning came, 185,000 Assyrian soldiers were dead.

One verse. That's all the writer gives it. No dramatic buildup. No extended battle scene. Just a single, devastating sentence. Sennacherib broke camp and went home to Nineveh. Twenty years later, while worshiping in the temple of his god, two of his own sons assassinated him. Every detail Isaiah had predicted came true.

The army that no nation could stop was stopped by a God no army could fight.

FIFTEEN MORE YEARS

Chapter 20 actually takes us back in time, to a period before Sennacherib's invasion. Hezekiah became deathly ill. The prophet Isaiah came to him with a grim message: "Put your house in order, because you are going to die."

Hezekiah turned his face to the wall and prayed. He wept bitterly and reminded God of his faithfulness. Before Isaiah had even left the middle court of the palace, God sent him back with a different word: "I have heard your prayer. I have seen your tears. I will heal you. On the third day you will go up to the temple of the Lord. I will add fifteen years to your life."

God's first word sounded final. But Hezekiah's prayer changed the outcome. Not because prayer manipulates God, but because God sometimes uses hard words as an invitation to come to him. Isaiah prescribed a treatment of figs applied to the boil, and Hezekiah recovered. God even gave him a miraculous sign, causing a shadow to move backward on a set of steps, confirming his promise.

It's a story of remarkable compassion. God heard. God saw. God healed. The king who trusted found that the God he trusted was tender enough to respond to tears.

THE VISITORS FROM BABYLON

But the story doesn't end there. After Hezekiah recovered, envoys arrived from Babylon. Merodach-Baladan, the Babylonian king, sent letters and a gift, apparently to congratulate Hezekiah on his recovery. In reality, he was shopping for allies against Assyria.

Hezekiah was flattered. Important people from a faraway empire were interested in him. So he gave them the full tour. He showed them everything: the silver, the gold, the spices, the fine oil, his entire armory, everything in his storehouses. The text emphasizes it twice: "There was nothing in his palace or in all his kingdom that Hezekiah did not show them."

Isaiah showed up and asked two pointed questions: "What did those men say? Where did they come from?" And then: "What did they see in your house?" Hezekiah answered honestly: "They saw everything."

Isaiah delivered God's verdict: "The time will surely come when everything in your palace, and all that your ancestors have stored up until this day, will be carried off to Babylon. Nothing will be left. And some of your own descendants will be taken away and will become servants in the palace of the king of Babylon."

The very nation Hezekiah was showing off to would one day return and take it all. The treasure tour was a preview of the plunder to come. The king who had trusted God against Assyria had leaned on Babylon instead, and it would cost his descendants everything.

Hezekiah's response was submissive but troubling: "The word of the Lord you have spoken is good." Some read his next thought as selfish: at least there will be peace and security in my lifetime. Others see it as an acknowledgment of God's mercy in delaying the judgment. Either way, the shadow of Babylon now hung over everything.

WHAT THIS MEANS FOR US

First, real faith doesn't prevent real suffering. Hezekiah was the most faithful king Judah ever had, and Assyria still invaded his country and devastated his land. Faith is not a shield against all trouble. It is the thing that sustains you in the middle of trouble. If you expect following God to make your life easy, you will be disappointed. If you expect God to be with you in the hardest moments, you will find him there.

Second, how you talk to God in a crisis matters. Hezekiah's prayer in the temple was not a panicked scream. He began by naming who God is. He acknowledged the truth of his situation. He asked for help not just for himself but for God's glory. When everything is falling apart, the discipline of starting your prayers with the truth about God anchors you to something that isn't shaking.

Third, God responds to honest prayer. When Hezekiah was told he would die, he prayed and wept, and God changed the outcome. When Sennacherib threatened Jerusalem, Hezekiah prayed, and God destroyed the Assyrian army. Prayer is not a ritual. It is a conversation with a God who listens, who sees tears, and who acts.

Fourth, today's carelessness becomes tomorrow's catastrophe. Hezekiah trusted God against Assyria but showed off to Babylon. It seemed harmless at the time. But that moment of pride and political calculation planted the seed for the exile that would come generations later. The choices we make in seasons of comfort can have consequences that outlast us.

TALKING POINTS

1. **Hezekiah destroyed the bronze serpent Moses had made because people were worshiping it.** What does that tell us about the difference between respecting tradition and turning it into an idol? Are there good things in your life that might be pulling your attention away from God?

2. **The Rabshakeh tried to convince Jerusalem that their God couldn't save them.** What are some arguments people use today to try to shake your confidence in God? How can we respond to those arguments the way Hezekiah did?

3. **Hezekiah's prayer focused on who God is before asking for what he needed.** Why do you think starting with worship helps us pray better? How might reminding yourself of God's character change the way you handle fear or stress?

4. **God told Hezekiah he was going to die, and Hezekiah prayed for more time and received it.** What does this teach us about how prayer works? Does it mean we can always change God's mind, or is something deeper going on?

5. **Hezekiah showed the Babylonian envoys everything in his treasury. Isaiah said it would all be carried to Babylon someday.** What warning does this carry about pride and the desire to impress people? How can we stay humble when things are going well?

Hezekiah was the best king Judah ever had, and even he stumbled. His faith was genuine, his reforms were real, his prayers were heard. But the road to Babylon had been opened, and after Hezekiah came a king so wicked that God's patience with Judah would finally reach its limit. The brightest light in Judah's history was about to be followed by its deepest darkness.

Turn the page.

8

THE LONG FALL

In *Toy Story 3*, the toys end up on a conveyor belt heading toward a furnace. They've been through a lot by this point. They've been abandoned, imprisoned, and betrayed. Now they're sliding toward an incinerator, and there is absolutely nothing they can do about it. One by one, they stop struggling. Woody. Buzz. Jessie. They reach for each other's hands. They don't say anything. They just hold on. It is the darkest moment in any Pixar film, maybe the darkest moment in any animated movie ever made. You sit there watching and thinking: This can't be how it ends. Not like this.

Second Kings 21–25 is that conveyor belt. After Hezekiah's faithfulness and God's miraculous rescue of Jerusalem, you might expect the story to get better. It doesn't. What comes next is the worst king Judah ever had, followed by a brief and brilliant reformation that arrives too late, followed by the total destruction of Jerusalem and the exile of God's people to Babylon.

These chapters are hard to read. But they are honest. And buried in the wreckage, almost invisible unless you know where to look, there is something that refuses to die. A whisper. A name. A promise that not even Babylon can extinguish.

THE WORST KING

Manasseh was twelve years old when he became king, and he reigned for fifty-five years. That makes him the longest-reigning king in the history of either Israel or Judah. It also makes him the most destructive.

Everything Hezekiah had torn down, Manasseh rebuilt. He re-erected the high places. He built altars to Baal. He made an image of the goddess Asherah and put it inside the temple of the Lord, the very building where God had promised to place his name forever. He constructed altars to the stars and planets in the courts of the temple. He practiced sorcery and divination. He consulted mediums and spiritists.

And he sacrificed his own son in the fire.

The writer of Kings doesn't compare Manasseh to the bad kings of Judah. He compares him to the pagan nations God had driven out of the land before Israel arrived. Manasseh had out-paganized the pagans. He "led Judah astray, so that they did more evil than the nations the Lord had destroyed before the Israelites."

Verse 16 adds one more horror: "Moreover, Manasseh also shed so much innocent blood that he filled Jerusalem from end to end." We don't get names or details. But the tradition preserved in other Jewish writings says that among those Manasseh killed was the prophet Isaiah himself. Whether or not that specific claim is true, the picture is clear. Anyone who opposed

Manasseh's agenda was eliminated. Prophets, priests, faithful believers. The blood ran through the streets of the holy city.

And God responded. Through his prophets, he announced that because of what Manasseh had done, Jerusalem would suffer the same fate as Samaria. God would stretch out over Jerusalem the same measuring line of destruction he had used on the northern kingdom. He would wipe Jerusalem clean like someone wiping a dish and turning it upside down. He would hand his people over to their enemies.

This was the point of no return. Later, even after Josiah's extraordinary reforms, the writer will circle back to this verdict: "Nevertheless, the Lord did not turn away from the heat of his fierce anger, which burned against Judah because of all that Manasseh had done to provoke him to anger." Manasseh's sin didn't just hurt his own generation. It poisoned the future. The judgment that would eventually fall on Jerusalem in 587 BC was, in the writer's view, sealed during Manasseh's reign.

Manasseh died and was buried. His son Amon followed him and lasted two years before his own servants assassinated him. But "the people of the land" executed the conspirators and placed Amon's eight-year-old son on the throne.

That boy's name was Josiah.

THE KING WHO CAME TOO LATE

Josiah is one of the most remarkable figures in the entire Bible. The writer says he did what was right in the eyes of the Lord and "walked in all the ways of his father David, not turning aside to the right or to the left." He shares that superlative with only Hezekiah. He was everything a king of Judah was supposed to be.

In his eighteenth year, Josiah ordered repairs to the temple. During the renovation, the high priest Hilkiah discovered something that had apparently been lost or hidden: the Book of the Law. Most scholars believe this was the book of Deuteronomy, or a large portion of it. When Josiah heard the words read aloud, he tore his robes in anguish. He understood immediately that Judah had been violating God's covenant for generations. The curses written in that book were aimed directly at them.

Josiah sent a delegation to the prophetess Huldah to ask what God intended to do. Her answer was two-sided. First, the bad news: judgment was coming. God's anger had been kindled against Judah, and it would not be quenched. The disaster announced against Jerusalem was certain. Second, the personal mercy: because Josiah's heart was tender, because he had humbled himself and wept before God when he heard the words of the Law, he would be spared. He would die in peace and would not see the catastrophe with his own eyes.

Josiah knew the nation was doomed. He pressed ahead with reform anyway. He gathered all the people of Judah and read the entire Book of the Law to them in the temple courts. He renewed the covenant, pledging to follow the Lord and keep his commands with all his heart and soul. Then he launched the most thorough religious purge in Judah's history.

He cleaned out the temple, removing every pagan vessel and idol. He tore down the quarters where male prostitutes had operated inside the temple complex. He desecrated the high places throughout the countryside. He demolished the altar at Bethel, the same one Jeroboam had built over three hundred years earlier, fulfilling a prophecy spoken by an unnamed prophet all the way back in 1 Kings 13. He celebrated a Passover so faithful to Scripture that the writer says nothing like it had been observed since the days of the judges.

And none of it was enough. After listing all of Josiah's reforms in breathtaking detail, after calling him a king without equal, the writer delivers the most heartbreaking verses in the book: "Nevertheless, the Lord did not turn away from the heat of his fierce anger. For Manasseh had provoked him beyond all that could be recovered."

Josiah did everything right. It still didn't save the nation. The damage was too deep. The rot had gone too far. And the reader is left with a staggering truth: there is such a thing as too late. Not too late for an individual to repent. Josiah himself found mercy. But too late for a nation to reverse the accumulated consequences of generations of rebellion.

Josiah died in 609 BC in a needless battle against Pharaoh Necho of Egypt. With his death, the last restraint on Judah's fall was removed.

FOUR KINGS AND A FUNERAL

What followed was a rapid, sickening collapse. Four kings ruled Judah after Josiah, and the writer dispatches each of them with the same blunt verdict: "He did evil in the eyes of the Lord."

Jehoahaz lasted three months. Pharaoh Necho deposed him and carried him off to Egypt, installing his brother Jehoiakim as a puppet king. Jehoiakim ruled for eleven years. He was arrogant, cruel, and utterly godless. The prophet Jeremiah describes him building a lavish palace with unpaid labor while the nation crumbled around him. When Jeremiah's prophecies were read to him, Jehoiakim sliced the scroll apart with a knife and burned it piece by piece in his fireplace. He murdered at least one prophet who spoke against him. When Nebuchadnezzar of Babylon conquered the region, Jehoiakim submitted, then foolishly rebelled. He died before the full consequences arrived.

His son Jehoiachin inherited the disaster. He was eighteen years old and reigned three months before Nebuchadnezzar besieged Jerusalem in 597 BC. Jehoiachin surrendered. Nebuchadnezzar stripped the temple and palace of their treasures, cut up the gold articles Solomon had made, and deported ten thousand of Judah's best people to Babylon: soldiers, craftsmen, officials, and the king himself. Among the exiles was a young priest named Ezekiel, who would become one of the greatest prophets in Israel's history.

Nebuchadnezzar placed Jehoiachin's uncle Zedekiah on the throne. Zedekiah would be the last king of Judah. The writer says he did evil in the eyes of the Lord, just like Jehoiakim. But where Jehoiakim had been viciously stubborn, Zedekiah was spineless. He couldn't make a decision and stick with it. Jeremiah pleaded with him repeatedly to submit to Babylon and save the city. Zedekiah would listen, seem to agree, and then reverse course as soon as his advisors pressured him. Eventually he rebelled against Nebuchadnezzar, and Babylon came back for the last time.

THE FIRE

In January of 588 BC, Nebuchadnezzar's army arrived at the walls of Jerusalem and began a siege that would last a year and a half. By the summer of 587, the famine inside the city was so severe that there was no food left for the people. The city wall was breached on the ninth day of the fourth month.

Zedekiah tried to escape at night with his soldiers, slipping out through a gate near the king's garden. The Babylonians caught him on the plains of Jericho. His army scattered. They brought him to Nebuchadnezzar at Riblah, where the Babylonian king pronounced judgment. Zedekiah's sons were killed in front of him. Then his eyes were put out. The last thing the last king of Judah ever saw was the death of his own children. They bound him in chains and carried him to Babylon.

A month later, Nebuzaradan, the commander of Nebuchadnezzar's guard, arrived in Jerusalem to finish the job. He burned the temple of the Lord. He burned the royal palace. He burned every important building in the city. His soldiers tore down the walls. The remaining population was deported to Babylon. Only the poorest people in the land were left behind to work the vineyards and fields.

The writer lingers over the destruction of the temple. He describes the bronze pillars, the great bronze basin, the stands, the pots, the shovels, the wick trimmers, the dishes, the sprinkling bowls, all of it carried away or broken up and hauled to Babylon. He describes the height of the pillars, the bronze capitals on top of them, the decorative network and pomegranates. It reads almost like a eulogy. He wants you to feel what was lost. This was the house Solomon had built, the place where God's glory had descended in a cloud so thick that the priests couldn't stand to minister. Now it was ash.

The Babylonians appointed a governor named Gedaliah

over the few who remained. For a brief moment it looked like life might stabilize. But within months, a man named Ishmael, who was of royal blood, assassinated Gedaliah along with the Jews and Babylonian soldiers stationed with him. The surviving population, terrified of Babylonian retaliation, fled to Egypt. The land God had promised to Abraham, the land Joshua had conquered, the land David had ruled, was empty.

A WHISPER IN BABYLON

The book of 2 Kings could have ended there. Smoke rising from the ruins. Exiles trudging toward Babylon. An empty land. A broken covenant. A story that began with Elijah ascending in a chariot of fire ending with the temple descending into actual fire.

But the writer adds four more verses.

In the thirty-seventh year of Jehoiachin's exile, a new king came to power in Babylon. His name was Evil-Merodach. In his first year, he released Jehoiachin from prison. He spoke kindly to him. He gave him a seat of honor above all the other exiled kings in Babylon. Jehoiachin exchanged his prison clothes for new garments. For the rest of his life, he ate at the king's table. He received a regular allowance, day by day, for as long as he lived.

It doesn't sound like much. An aging prisoner gets a promotion in a foreign court. But look closer.

Jehoiachin is called "king of Judah." Twice. Even in Babylon, even after everything, the writer insists on that title. The line of David has not been erased. The man sitting at that Babylonian table carries the blood of the covenant in his veins.

And if you trace that bloodline forward through the centuries, past the return from exile, past the rebuilding of the temple, past the long silence between the testaments, you arrive at a man named Joseph who was descended from David through the line of Jehoiachin. And Joseph was the legal father of Jesus.

The promise didn't die in Babylon. It was just waiting.

WHAT THIS MEANS FOR US

First, sin has consequences that outlast the sinner. Manasseh repented late in life, according to 2 Chronicles. But his repentance couldn't undo fifty-five years of damage. The idolatry he planted took root so deep that even Josiah's heroic reforms couldn't pull it all out. The choices we make don't just affect us. They shape the people who come after us. That should make us take our influence seriously.

Second, faithfulness matters even when it doesn't "work." Josiah knew the nation was doomed. He reformed anyway. Not because reform would save Judah, but because God deserved to be obeyed whether it produced visible results or not. Sometimes doing the right thing doesn't fix the situation. Do it anyway. God doesn't measure obedience by outcomes. He measures it by faithfulness.

Third, God's judgment is real and should be taken seriously. The fall of Jerusalem wasn't an accident of politics. It was the fulfillment of warnings God had been issuing for centuries through his prophets. The writer of Kings wants us to understand that when God says something will happen, it happens. His promises of blessing are reliable. So are his warnings of judgment.

Fourth, even in the darkest ending, God preserves a thread of hope. Jehoiachin in Babylon is not a triumphant conclusion. It's a whisper. But it's a whisper that says the line of David is still alive, God's promise is still intact, and the story is not over. The God who began this story with Abraham is not finished. He is never finished.

TALKING POINTS

1. **Manasseh reigned for fifty-five years and did immense damage.** Why do you think God allowed such a wicked king to rule for so long? What does this teach us about the mystery of God's timing and patience?

2. **Josiah discovered the Book of the Law and was devastated by what he read.** What does his reaction tell us about the kind of heart God values? How can we develop that same sensitivity to God's word in our own lives?

3. **Josiah kept obeying even after he knew the nation was doomed.** What would it feel like to serve God knowing your efforts wouldn't change the outcome? Why is that kind of obedience valuable to God?

4. **The writer describes the destruction of the temple in painful detail.** Why do you think he lingered over those descriptions instead of summarizing them quickly? What was he trying to make his readers feel?

5. **The book ends with Jehoiachin eating at a king's table in Babylon. It doesn't seem like much of a happy ending.** But how does knowing that Jesus came from Jehoiachin's line change the way you read those final verses? What does it teach us about how God keeps his promises?

The temple is in ashes. The walls are rubble. The people are scattered. And an old man sits at a table in Babylon, eating bread from a foreign king's kitchen, wearing clothes that are not his own.

But he is alive. And he is a son of David.

That is how the book of 2 Kings ends. Not with a victory parade. Not with a restored kingdom. With a whisper of survival in the wreckage. A heartbeat where there should have been silence. A thread of promise so thin it could snap at any moment, except that the God holding the other end has never once let go.

The story of 2 Kings is the story of what happens when people walk away from God. It is full of warnings and judgments and kings who should have known better. But it is also the story of a God who keeps showing up. Who sends prophets when no one wants to listen. Who preserves a baby in a temple closet when a queen is murdering the royal family. Who shatters an army in a single night because a king had the courage to pray. Who hides his promise in the bloodline of an exiled prisoner and waits, patiently and stubbornly, for the right moment to fulfill it.

That moment came in a stable in Bethlehem, in a town that belonged to the family of David, when a child was born who would be everything Hezekiah and Josiah and every other king had failed to be. A king who would not stumble. A king who would not compromise. A king whose kingdom would have no end.

The book of 2 Kings is finished. But the story it tells is still being written. And the King it points to is still on his throne.

www.ingramcontent.com/pod-product-compliance
Ingram Content Group UK Ltd.
Pitfield, Milton Keynes, MK11 3LW, UK
UKHW020420250726
13967UKWH00007B/2741

9 781971 767185